Dimensions of Ethnicity

A Series of Selections from the
Harvard Encyclopedia of American Ethnic Groups

Stephan Thernstrom, *Editor*
Ann Orlov, *Managing Editor*
Oscar Handlin, *Consulting Editor*

Immigration

Richard A. Easterlin
David Ward
William S. Bernard
Reed Ueda

The Belknap Press of
Harvard University Press
Cambridge, Massachusetts
London, England
1982

Library of Congress Cataloging in Publication Data

Main entry under title:

Immigration.

> (Dimensions of ethnicity)
> Selections from the Harvard encyclopedia of American ethnic groups.
> Bibliography: p.
> Contents: Economic and social characteristics of the immigrants / Richard A. Easterlin—Settlement patterns and spatial distribution / David Ward—A history of U.S. immigration policy / William S. Bernard—[etc.]
> 1. United States—Emigration and immigration—History—Addresses, essays, lectures.   I. Easterlin, Richard Ainley, 1926-   . II. Series.

JV6450.I557   1982   325.73   82–6124
ISBN 0–674–44439–6 (pbk.)   AACR2

Foreword

Ethnicity is a central theme—perhaps the central theme—of American history. From the first encounters between Englishmen and Indians at Jamestown down to today's "boat people," the interplay between peoples of differing national origins, religions, and races has shaped the character of our national life. Although scholars have long recognized this fact, in the past two decades they have paid it more heed than ever before. The result has been an explosive increase in research on America's complex ethnic mosaic. Examination of a recent bibliography of doctoral dissertations on ethnic themes written between 1899 and 1972 reveals that no less than half of them appeared in the years 1962–1972. The pace of inquiry has not slackened since then; it has accelerated.

The extraordinary proliferation of literature on ethnicity and ethnic groups made possible—and necessary—an effort to take stock. An authoritative, up-to-date synthesis of the current state of knowledge in the field was called for. The *Harvard Encyclopedia of American Ethnic Groups*, published by the Harvard University Press in 1980, is such a synthesis. It provides entries by leading scholars on the origins, history, and present situation of the more than 100 ethnic groups that make up the population of the United States, and 29 thematic essays on a wide range of ethnic topics. As one reviewer said, the volume is "a kind of *summa ethnica* of our time."

I am pleased that some of the most interesting and valuable articles in the encyclopedia are now available to a wider audience through inexpensive paperback editions such as this one. These essays will be an excellent starting point for anyone in search of deeper understanding of who the American people are and how they came to be that way.

Stephan Thernstrom

Contents

1

ECONOMIC AND SOCIAL CHARACTERISTICS OF THE IMMIGRANTS

The magnitude of immigration to America is unmatched in the history of mankind. This article sketches the overall dimensions of the flow, its origins abroad and destinations within the United States, and the characteristics of the migrants. It also examines the causes of immigration and its effects on the increase in population, total economic output, and output per head.

Dimensions

Trends and Fluctuations

Since the settlement of Jamestown in 1607, well over 45 million people have immigrated to the present area of the United States. Not all of them stayed; for the period from 1810 onward, when the magnitude of the movement can be gauged more accurately, a rough estimate of the volume of net immigration, the excess of arriving immigrants over departing emigrants, is about 38 million.

Relatively few immigrants came to the United States in the first third of the 19th century (see Table 1.1). In the 1830s a

Table 1.1. Increase in U.S. population by component of change, 1810–1970 (thousands per decade).

Period	Total increase	Natural increase[a]	Net arrivals[b]
1810–1820	2,399	2,328	71
1821–1830	3,228	3,105	123
1831–1840	4,203	3,710	493
1841–1850	6,122	4,702	1,420
1851–1860	8,251	5,614	2,593
1861–1870	8,375	6,291	2,102
1871–1880	10,337	7,675	2,622
1881–1890	12,792	7,527	4,966
1891–1900	13,047	9,345	3,711
1901–1910	15,978	9,656	6,294
1911–1920	13,738	11,489	2,484
1921–1930	17,604	14,500	3,187
1931–1940	8,894	9,962	−85
1941–1950	19,028	17,666	1,362
1951–1960	28,626	25,446	3,180
1961–1970	23,912	19,894	4,018

Source: Conrad Taeuber and Irene Taeuber, *The Changing Population of the United States* (New York, 1958), p. 294, table 91; U.S. Bureau of the Census, *Historical Statistics of the United States: Colonial Times to 1970* (Washington, D.C., 1975), pp. 8, 49.
   a. Excess of births over deaths.
   b. Excess of immigrants arrivals over departures. Estimated natural increase and estimated net arrivals do not coincide precisely with total increase figures because of imperfect data for births, deaths, and immigration.

notable increase began which, with some interruptions, persisted until the first decade of the 20th century, when more than 6 million newcomers arrived. World War I and the restrictive legislation of the 1920s brought this trend to a halt: immigration fell to 2 to 3 million people per decade between 1910 and 1930, and plummeted during the Great Depression;

in the 1930s, for the first time in its history, the United States actually lost more people through migration than it gained. Since World War II a considerable net influx has resumed, amounting to about 3 million people in the 1950s and 4 million in both the 1960s and 1970s.

Although immigration to the United States has been of unprecedented size, its actual contribution to the total increase of population has been smaller, and often considerably smaller, than natural increase from the excess of births over deaths. Even in 1900–1910, the decade of peak immigration, immigration accounted for less than 40 percent of the total population increase. This appraisal is somewhat deceptive, however, for it fails to allow for the contribution to population growth from the second and later generations, which is counted in the natural increase figures. Later an attempt will be made to provide a more accurate notion of the contribution of immigration to the increase of total population in the period since 1790.

Absolute numbers do not tell the whole story. An influx of 1 million newcomers obviously has quite different significance depending on whether they join a population of 2 million or 200 million. The rate of immigration is the number of immigrants relative to the number of people already living in the area. Figure 1.1 presents the annual rate of immigration, the number of immigrants in each year per 1,000 total population in the United States at that time. The rate of immigration, like the absolute number of immigrants, starts at low levels in the second and third decades of the 19th century, and then begins to rise noticeably in the 1830s. But from the 1840s through World War I the trend in the rate of immigration differs from that in numbers of immigrants. Whereas the number continues to rise, the rate of immigration stays at a fairly constant average level (though fluctuating), because the rise in the volume of immigration after the 1840s was no more rapid than the growth of the U.S. population as a whole. Moreover, the volume of 3 to 4 million

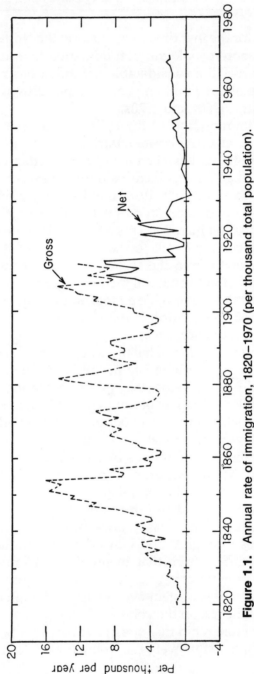

Figure 1.1. Annual rate of immigration, 1820–1970 (per thousand total population).
Source: Richard A. Easterlin, *Population, Labor Force, and Long Swings in Economic Growth: The American Experience* (New York, 1968), pp. 204–209; U.S. Bureau of the Census, *Historical Statistics of the United States, from Colonial Times to 1970* (Washington D.C., 1975), pp. 8, 113.

people entering in each decade since 1950, though comparable in absolute numbers to the amount in the late 19th century, is much less significant relative to the current population of the United States. In that respect the restrictive legislation of the 1920s achieved its purpose.

Because the data plotted in Figure 1.1 are yearly, they reveal other features of the temporal pattern of immigration. First, there are noticeable year-to-year fluctuations which turn out to be associated with the business cycle. Economic expansions generated a rise in immigration, and contractions a decline, with a brief lag for the time it took information about new circumstances to cross the ocean. Second, these shorter-term fluctuations are dwarfed by a longer-term movement, usually of around 15 to 20 years' duration, which is apparent in the figures from around 1840 to 1940. Peak immigration periods in these "long swings" occur around 1851–1854, 1866–1873, 1881–1883, 1905–1907, and 1921–1924. The dampening effect of restrictive legislation on both short- and long-term fluctuations is strikingly evident in the years after 1924.

In principle, the history of American immigration, together with that of the importation of slaves, dates from the founding of Jamestown, and is in a sense virtually coterminous with the history of the entire American population, except for the American Indians. It is customary, however, to distinguish colonial settlers and their descendants, the "colonial stock," from those who arrived after the establishment of an independent United States. Unfortunately, less is known of immigration in the colonial period. Records of immigration to the various colonies, to the extent that they exist at all, are uneven and spotty, and have yet to be systematically assembled and studied. For these reasons, this essay focuses on immigration after 1790, and especially during the period of free immigration, when the flow was at a maximum. Discussion will be confined to voluntary migration, and will not treat the enforced migration of slaves, an important but quite different subject.

Colonial Immigration

A few general observations can be made regarding immigration in the colonial period. First, the absolute number of immigrants was much lower than in the 19th century: the cumulative total of immigrants over the 16 decades from 1630 to 1790 was well under 1 million. In contrast, in each decade between 1850 and 1930 net immigration ranged between 2 and over 6 million. Second, although the number of immigrants was substantially higher in the 18th than in the 17th century, most of the population in 1790 was native-born; natural increase was the principal source of its dramatically high growth rate. Third, the rate of immigration was high in the first half of the 17th century. By the 18th century the rate had fallen to an average level considerably lower than in the mid- and late 19th century: a reasonable contrast might be between, say, 2 per thousand and 10 per thousand. Finally, as in the later period, colonial migration was characterized by long-term swings—upsurges and declines—although more data are needed before these movements can be dated adequately.

Sex, Age, and Marital Status

Although people came to the United States for a variety of reasons, the primary impulse was for economic betterment. As a result, throughout the period of free immigration, a substantial majority of the newcomers were those whose services were most in demand, single males of prime working age. For most of the 19th century, males comprised about 60 percent of the total, and people aged 15–39, about two-thirds. In the two to three decades before World War I, the period of the "New Immigration" (see the discussion of national origins below), the dominance of prime working age males grew. The proportion male rose to around 67 percent and the proportion aged 15–39 climbed to about three-fourths.

Data are not available on the marital status of immigrants in the 19th century, but is seems likely that half or more were single. In the first decade of the 20th century the majority of immigrants—approximately 60 percent—were single.

The laws restricting immigration after World War I brought noticeable changes in the demographic characteristics of immigrants. Least affected was age composition; those of prime working age continued to predominate, although even their share in the total dropped, chiefly at the expense of younger persons: those aged 15–44 composed somewhat over 60 percent of the total in the 1960s. However, females became the dominant group for the first time in history, accounting for a majority of immigrants in every year since 1930. This trend reflects humanitarian concerns in the new laws—the priority given to family reunions as a criterion for immigration, and the importance of refugee or quasi-refugee movements. Closely related was a shift in marital status: married immigrants accounted for a slight majority in most years after 1930.

Literacy

Immigrants have sometimes been characterized as a largely illiterate group, but the evidence available does not support this view. Information on literacy upon arrival in the United States began to be collected in 1899. Because these data cover the period of the "New Immigration," when illiteracy allegedly was highest, they are of particular interest. The concept of literacy is described in the 1910 report of the U.S. Immigration Commission, a special congressional committee established to investigate immigration problems, as follows:

> Immigrants when seeking admission to the United States are not tested as to their ability to read and write, and the data upon this point represent the statements of such immigrants in answer to the inquiries, "Can you read?" and "Can you write?" The assurance of the im-

migrant that he is able to read or write in some language or dialect is accepted as proof of literacy. Of course, data secured by this method are not absolutely conclusive, but as the inquiries quoted are simple in character, and as the immigrant's educational status in no way affects his right to admission, it may be assumed that the information obtained is substantially accurate.

Table 1.2, based upon the commission's report, summarizes the data for 1899–1910. Two features are notewor-

Table 1.2. Immigrants admitted to the United States, 14 years and older, who could neither read nor write, 1899–1910, by race or people

Race or people	Number admitted	Persons who could neither read nor write	
		Number	Percent
Portuguese	55,930	38,122	68.2
Turkish	12,670	7,536	59.5
Mexican	32,721	18,717	57.2
Italian, South	1,690,376	911,566	53.9
Ruthenian (Russniak)[a]	140,775	75,165	53.4
Syrian	47,834	25,496	53.3
Lithuanian	161,441	79,001	48.9
East Indian	5,724	2,703	47.2
Bulgarian, Serbian, and Montenegrin	95,596	39,903	41.7
Dalmatian, Bosnian, and Herzegovinian	30,861	12,653	41.0
Russian	77,479	29,777	38.4
Korean	7,259	2,763	38.1
Croatian and Slovenian	320,977	115,785	36.1
Polish	861,303	304,675	35.4
Romanian	80,839	28,266	35.0

Table 1.2   (*Continued*)

Race or people	Number admitted	Persons who could neither read nor write	
		Number	Percent
Greek	208,608	55.089	26.4
Hebrew	806,786	209,507	26.0
Pacific Islander	336	83	24.7
Japanese	146,172	35,956	24.6
Slovak	342,583	82,216	24.0
Armenian	23,523	5,624	23.9
African (black)	30,177	5,733	19.0
Spanish	46,418	6,724	14.5
Italian, North	339,301	38,897	11.5
Magyar (incl. Hungarian)	307,082	35,004	11.4
Chinese	21,584	1,516	7.0
Cuban	36,431	2,282	6.3
French	97,638	6,145	6.3
Spanish-American	9,008	547	6.1
German	625,793	32,236	5.2
Dutch and Flemish	68,907	3,043	4.4
West Indian (except Cuban)	9,983	320	3.2
Irish	416,640	10,721	2.6
Welsh	17,076	322	1.9
Bohemian and Moravian[b]	79,721	1,322	1.7
Finnish	137,916	1,745	1.3
English	347,458	3,647	1.0
Scots	115,788	767	0.7
Scandinavian	530,634	2,221	0.4
Other peoples	11,209	5,001	44.6
Not specified	67	5	7.5
Total	8,398,624	2,238,801	26.7

Source: U.S. Senate, 61st Congress, 3rd Session, Doc. No. 747, Reports of the Immigration Commission, *Abstracts of Reports of the Immigration Commission* (Washington, D.C., 1911), p. 99.
   a. Ruthenians are Carpatho-Rusyns.
   b. Bohemians and Moravians are from present-day Czechoslovakia.

thy: almost three-quarters of immigrants in this period reported themselves as able to read or write; and there were immense disparities among the different ethnic groups. Generally speaking, literacy was highest among people from northern and western Europe and lowest among those from southern and eastern Europe. Even for those from the latter areas, however, there were only a few groups among whom illiterates were a majority.

These data are consistent with those from another source, enumerations of the foreign-born obtained in the general census of the U.S. population taken every ten years. The census definition of literacy was essentially the same as that given above, but because the data do not refer to the date of immigration, they reflect improvements in the education of immigrants that occurred after their arrival. From the first census literacy count in 1880 over 85 percent of the foreign-born reported themselves as literate. Although literacy was slightly higher among the native-born, the difference was not very great. In considering the commission and census records it is useful to bear in mind that literacy could and probably often did refer to the native language of an immigrant, and that in many parts of northwestern Europe the development of formal school systems dated from the first part of the 19th century. It should also be remembered that a large share of the American-born population was from rural origins, and that schooling was less developed in rural than in urban areas.

The absolute number of immigrants in 1899–1910 who reported themselves illiterate—2.2 million—is sizable, and if, as was doubtless the case, they were largely concentrated in a few urban centers, it would have been easy for some native Americans to gain the impression that immigrants were generally illiterate. Moreover, even those who were literate at time of entry often did not speak English, and native Americans might well have thought of literacy in those terms. There are no figures on English-speaking ability at time of entry. The census data for 1890–1930, however, revealed the following percentages of foreign-born unable to speak English: 1890, 15.6; 1900, 12.2; 1910, 22.8; 1920, 11.0; 1930, 6.6. These data imply that even if a considerable number of immigrants did not know English at the time of entry, they acquired some knowledge in a fairly short time. Walter Willcox concluded that "the figures indicate that between seven-tenths and nine-tenths of the non-English-speaking immigrants had learned or claimed to have learned English between the time of arrival and a subsequent census."

The data do not mean that as a general matter most immigrants became highly fluent in English. They do suggest, however, that many immigrants had had some rudiments of formal education in their native land and picked up enough English to manage in the United States. Immigrants to the United States were not generally from the least literate ranks in their areas of origin. This makes sense, for immigrant families had to surmount the difficulties of travel and relocation to a foreign land, and a certain level of language competence was essential for this task.

Within the United States geographic differences in the extent of public schooling may account in part for the rapid linguistic assimilation of the immigrants. The South lagged noticeably behind the rest of the country. Estimates for whites in 1850 put school enrollment in the South at around six-tenths or less that in the rest of the United States, a differential that has persisted to the present, though in lesser magnitude. Schooling in urban areas has been significantly ahead of that in rural areas—data relating to literacy rates and educational attainment consistently show urban levels higher than rural. Immigrants generally avoided the South and were much more concentrated in urban areas than the American-born population. Consequently, their children, though not the immigrants themselves, generally acquired superior schooling to that available to the colonial stock.

National Origins

Where have the 45 million American immigrants come from? The answer varies depending on the time. In the colonial period virtually all immigrants were from northwestern Europe, the great majority of them from the British Isles. An estimate of the percentage distribution of the white population by nationality in 1790 shows:

British Isles		78.9
English	60.9	
Scottish	8.3	
Irish	9.7	
German		8.7
Dutch		3.4
French		1.7
Swedish		0.7
Unknown		6.6

These figures are based on a classification of surnames in the 1790 Census. Although most of this population had been born in the colonies, the impression the figures convey in regard to immigration is doubtless correct. English-speaking settlers were an overwhelming majority, with German and Dutch settlers, who accounted for most of the remaining immigration, a distant second.

The origins of immigrants from 1820 on are much better documented. As in the colonial period, throughout most of the 19th century northwestern Europe accounted for over two-thirds of U.S. immigration (see Table 1.3). However, the proportion of migrants from the British Isles, though sizable, was considerably reduced, and among them there was a much larger representation from Ireland (see Table 1.4). Germany and Scandinavia became increasingly important, together equaling or exceeding the British Isles in their contributions from the 1870s until World War I. In the 1890s southern and eastern Europe together became the major source of newcomers. To check this "New Immigration" was the central purpose of the restrictive quota laws of the 1920s. Earlier, immigration from Asia to the Pacific Coast had been effectively terminated by legislation and treaties which sought to stem the "yellow peril." Compared with other nations, the United States in the 19th century was indeed something of a "melting pot," though from an international, or even European, point of view the ingredients considered appropriate were rather narrowly defined.

The origins of immigrants from the 1920s on show clearly the impact of shifts in legislation restricting immigration. Through the 1940s there was considerable reversion toward the pattern in which northwestern Europe predominated as an area of origin—due to the national quotas of the 1920s legislation—and Canada also emerged as a strong contributor. (Data before 1900 on immigration from Canada do not permit satisfactory separation of Canadians from Europeans who were passing through.) More recently, however, in the Western Hemisphere, Mexico and the West Indies have become major sources—in 1961–1970 they surpassed Canada. Moreover, this does not take into account illegal immigration from Mexico, which is generally believed to have exceeded legal immigration in recent years. Also, in the same decade immigration from Asia accounted for the first time for over a tenth of the total, with substantial numbers of immigrants coming from the Philippines, Korea, India, Hong Kong, and Taiwan. Together, immigrants from Asia and areas in the Western Hemisphere other than Canada accounted for an unprecedented majority of the total in the 1960s.

Rates of Emigration from European Countries

Tables 1.3 and 1.4 present the relative importance of various areas in terms of the absolute number of U.S. immigrant arrivals. It is also of interest to consider migration in relation to the size of the population in the area of origin. A small country necessarily contributes a small absolute number of migrants; yet this number may be large in relation to the potential number of migrants. Table 1.5 presents the available data on the average annual rate of overseas emigration for

Table 1.3. Distribution of total reported immigration, by continent, 1821–1970 (in percentages).[a]

Period	Total Europe	Europe North and west[b]	East and central[c]	South and other[d]	Western hemisphere	Asia	All other
1821–1830	69.2	67.1	—	2.1	8.4	—	22.4
1831–1840	82.8	81.8	—	1.0	5.5	—	11.7
1841–1850	93.3	92.9	0.1	0.3	3.6	—	3.1
1851–1860	94.4	93.6	0.1	0.8	2.9	1.6	1.1
1861–1870	89.2	87.8	0.5	0.9	7.2	2.8	0.8
1871–1880	80.8	73.6	4.5	2.7	14.4	4.4	0.4
1881–1890	90.3	72.0	11.9	6.3	8.1	1.3	0.3
1891–1900	96.5	44.5	32.8	19.1	1.1	1.9	0.5
1901–1910	92.5	21.7	44.5	26.3	4.1	2.8	0.6

Distribution by area of origin

1911–1920	76.3	17.4	33.4	25.5	19.9	3.4	0.4
1921–1930	60.3	31.7	14.4	14.3	36.9	2.4	0.4
1931–1940	65.9	38.8	11.0	16.1	30.3	2.8	0.9
1941–1950	60.1	47.5	4.6	7.9	34.3	3.1	2.5
1951–1960	52.8	17.7	24.3	10.8	39.6	6.0	1.6
1961–1970	34.0	11.7	9.4	12.9	51.7	12.7	1.7

Source: Conrad Taeuber and Irene Taeuber, The Changing Population of the United States (New York, 1958), p. 53, table 11; U.S. Bureau of the Census, Historical Statistics of the United States: Colonial Times to 1970 (Washington, D.C., 1975), pp. 105–109.

a. Figures for 1821–1867 represent alien passengers arriving in steerage; 1868–1891 and 1895–1897, immigrant aliens arriving; 1892–1894 and 1898–1970, immigrant aliens admitted; 1819–1868, by nationality; 1869–1898, by country of origin or nationality; 1899–1970, by country of last permanent residence.

b. Great Britain, Ireland, Norway, Sweden, Denmark, Iceland, Netherlands, Belgium, Luxembourg, Switzerland, France.

c. Germany (Austria included, 1938–1945), Poland, Czechoslovakia (since 1920), Yugoslavia (since 1920), Hungary (since 1861), Austria (since 1861, except 1938–1945), U.S.S.R. (excludes Asian U.S.S.R. between 1931 and 1963), Latvia, Estonia, Lithuania, Finland, Romania, Bulgaria, Turkey (in Europe).

d. Italy, Spain, Portugal, Greece, and other European countries not classified elsewhere.

Table 1.4. Major sources of immigrants from Europe and Western Hemisphere, by country, 1821–1970 (thousands per decade).[a]

Period	Great Britain	Ireland	Denmark, Norway, Sweden	Germany	Austria-Hungary	Russia	Italy	Canada	Mexico	West Indies
1821–1830	25	51	—	7	—	—	—	—	—	—
1831–1840	76	207	2	152	—	—	2	—	—	—
1841–1850	267	781	14	435	—	—	2	—	—	—
1851–1860	424	914	25	952	—	—	9	—	—	—
1861–1870	607	436	126	787	8	3	12	—	—	—
1871–1880	548	437	243	718	73	39	56	—	—	—
1881–1890	807	655	656	1,453	354	213	307	—	—	—
1891–1900	272	388	372	505	593	505	652	—	—	—
1901–1910	526	339	505	341	2,145	1,597	2,046	179	50	108
1911–1920	341	146	203	144	896	921	1,110	742	219	123
1921–1930	330	221	198	412	64	62	455	925	459	75
1931–1940	29	13	11	114	11	1	68	109	22	16
1941–1950	132	27	26	226	28	1	57	172	61	50
1951–1960	192	57	57	478	—	6	185	378	300	123
1961–1970	206	40	43	191	—	8	214	413	454	470
Total	4,782	4,712	2,481	6,915	4,172	3,356	5,175	2,918	1,565	965

Source: Conrad Taeuber and Irene Taeuber, *The Changing Population of the United States* (New York, 1958), p. 56, table 13; U.S. Bureau of the Census, *Historical Statistics of the United States: Colonial Times to 1970* (Washington, D.C., 1975), pp. 105–109.

a. Figures for 1821–1867 represent alien passengers arriving in steerage; 1868–1891 and 1895–1897, immigrant aliens arriving; 1892–1894 and 1896–1970, immigrant aliens admitted; 1819–1868 by nationality; 1869–1898, by country of origin or nationality; 1899–1970, by country of last permanent residence.

Table 1.5. Average annual rate of intercontinental emigration from Europe per decade, by country, 1821–1910.[a]

Country	1821–1830	1831–1840	1841–1850	1851–1860	1861–1870	1871–1880	1881–1890	1891–1900	1901–1910	Average 1861–1910[b]
Great Britain	0.7	1.5	2.8	3.8	3.1	4.1	5.9	3.7	6.5	4.6
Ireland	2.0	5.6	15.3	19.5	14.6	10.2	14.9	10.1	7.0	11.4
France	—	—	—	0.3	0.2	0.2	0.3	0.2	0.1	0.2
Belgium	—	—	—	0.1	0.2	0.2	0.6	0.3	0.6	0.3
Netherlands	—	—	—	0.5	0.6	0.5	1.2	0.5	0.5	0.7
Norway	—	—	—	2.4	5.8	4.7	9.6	4.5	8.3	6.6
Sweden	0.1	0.2	0.1	0.4	2.3	2.3	7.0	4.2	4.2	4.0
Denmark	—	—	—	0.2	1.1	2.0	3.9	2.2	2.8	2.4
Finland	—	—	—	—	—	0.3	1.2	2.4	5.4	2.1
Germany	—	—	1.7	2.6	1.7	1.5	2.9	1.0	0.4	1.5
Switzerland	—	—	—	1.0	1.4	1.3	3.1	1.4	1.4	1.7
Austria-Hungary	—	—	—	0.1	0.1	0.3	1.1	1.6	4.8	1.6
Portugal	—	—	—	—	1.9	2.9	3.8	5.1	5.7	3.8
Spain	—	—	—	—	—	—	2.2	2.1	5.7	—
Italy	—	—	—	—	1.0	1.0	3.2	4.9	10.8	4.1
Balkan states	—	—	—	—	—	—	0.1	0.2	1.6	—
Russia	—	—	—	—	0.0	0.1	0.3	0.5	1.6	0.5

Source: Walter F. Willcox, ed., *International Migrations,* I, *Statistics* (New York, 1929), pp. 229ff.; Gustav Sundbärg, *Aperçus Statistiques Internationaux* (New York, 1908).

a. Number of emigrants per year per thousand of the resident population in that year. Figures before 1851 are approximate.

b. Averages for Spain and the Balkan states are not available because figures for the period are incomplete.

the European countries per 1,000 population from 1821 to 1910. The data cover emigrants to all overseas areas, not just to the United States. However, because the United States absorbed the largest share of the migration (over two-thirds in the period 1861–1910), the data furnish a reasonable indication of which countries sent migrants to the United States at the highest rate.

Ireland had by far the largest rate of emigration. Among other areas in northwestern Europe, Scandinavia and Great Britain are next in importance. Italy, Portugal, and (if sufficient data were available) probably Spain had considerably higher rates of emigration between 1861 and 1910 than did Germany, Austria-Hungary, or Switzerland, reflecting the very high levels of emigration from southern Europe. France and the Low Countries had the lowest rates of emigration, along with Russia and the Balkan area. In general, aside from the last two areas, which entered the movement quite late, and Ireland, which experienced the catastrophic impact of the potato famine, rates of emigration tended to be higher the lower a country's level of economic development and the higher its rate of natural increase.

Geographic Distribution

Two great geographic movements have dominated the distribution of the American population. One was the steady westward expansion associated with the process of farm settlement, which had largely run its course by the end of the 19th century. The other is urbanization, which began to gather momentum in the first half of the 19th century as industrialization took hold, and continues, somewhat modified, to the present.

In the 19th century, immigrants, American-born whites, and blacks participated differently in the spatial redistribution of the population. Westward expansion was accomplished primarily by native whites. But in urban growth after 1840, especially the growth of large cities, immigrants and their descendants played a disproportionate part (although American-born whites dominated the more influential urban occupations). Blacks remained concentrated in southern agriculture and participated in its westward expansion. In the 20th century, as urban concentration emerged as the dominant geographic movement, the location and economic function of the three population groups grew increasingly similar, although important differences continued to exist between whites and nonwhites (immigrant or native-born).

The trends are demonstrated most clearly when the white population is divided into native and foreign "stock." The foreign stock includes foreign-born (or first-generation) immigrants, and their children, that is, native-born people with at least one foreign parent. Native stock in the United States is defined as native-born persons of American parentage, and includes the grandchildren and subsequent descendants of immigrants. By these definitions 55 percent of the U.S. population in 1890 was native white stock; 33 percent, foreign white stock; and 12 percent, nonwhite.

The extent to which these groups participated in agricultural settlement is roughly indicated by the composition of the rural population toward the end of the 19th century in the areas settled subsequent to independence. As of 1890 in the north-central and western regions, 62 percent of the rural population was native white stock; 37 percent, foreign white stock; and 1 percent, nonwhite. In the south central region, 67 percent was native white stock; 2 percent, foreign white stock; and 31 percent, nonwhite. Thus in both areas the native white stock was disproportionately represented. But there was an interesting contrast between North and South in the roles of foreign white stock and nonwhites. Outside the South, the foreign white stock accounted for almost all of the remaining rural population; within the South, the nonwhites did.

When one turns to the figures on urban population the role of the foreign stock becomes prominent. Although the foreign stock represented only a third of the U.S. population in 1890, it made up 53 percent of the urban population. Again, as in the case of the rural population, there was a striking difference between the South and the rest of the country in the presence of foreign stock and nonwhites. Nonwhites accounted for only 2 percent of the urban population outside the South, but for 33 percent within it. The proportion of the foreign white stock in urban areas in the South was less, although it amounted to almost a quarter of the urban population in that region. Because of the varying roles the three groups played in the geographic redistribution of the population, they exhibited important differences in location as of 1890, differences which were germane to the development of their attitudes and subsequent behavior. The native white stock was still an essentially rural and small-town group both inside and outside the South. Three out of four people in this group lived in rural areas, and only 8 percent were in cities of 100,000 or more. In contrast, the foreign white stock was predominantly urban (58 percent), and a substantial proportion—one person in three—lived in large cities. As of 1890, nine out of ten blacks remained in the South, and four out of five were in rural areas.

The 20th century witnessed a major revolution in these patterns, as the frontier closed and urban concentration became the dominant force shaping population distribution. The result was a dramatic change in the distribution of both the native white stock and the nonwhites. By 1960 almost two out of three people of native white stock lived in urban areas; for nonwhites the proportion was a little higher.

The growing urban concentration of the population has vastly multiplied the contacts among groups from different backgrounds. In the late 19th century the problem of assimilation of immigrants, especially those from southern and eastern Europe, began to be felt with increasing urgency. Cutting off the supply of immigrants through legislation discriminating on the basis of national origin made the problem more manageable. At the same time, education of the children of immigrants made it possible for them to move up the occupational scale, and fostered their assimilation. But the curtailment of the immigrant labor supply had domestic repercussions. Immigrants and nonwhites were to some extent alternative sources of labor: where one group was large, the other was typically small. With the foreign labor supply largely cut off around World War I, periods of high labor demand in the North began increasingly to generate large movements of blacks out of the South. World War I and the 1920s were the first of these periods. After an interruption during the Depression of the 1930s, this process was resumed during World War II and afterward. With this shift in the sources of labor supply, the problem of assimilating immigrants was transformed into that of integrating blacks and, in the last three decades, Hispanics.

Immigrants by Occupation

Occupations in Area of Origin

The impression that 19th-century immigrants were largely a displaced European peasantry finds only limited support in the data. Among those reporting occupations at time of entry, the dominant group by far is the unskilled category of general labor and domestic service, which accounted for about half of those reporting occupations in the period from 1851 through World War I (see Table 1.6). Those reporting an agricultural occupation accounted in most decades for around one-fourth or less of the total, not much more than those reporting occupations in industry and mining—a nonfarm manual labor group. Of course there were important differences by area of origin. For example, in 1899–1915 the proportion of non-Jewish immigrants from southern and eastern Europe reporting an agricultural occupation was one-third, while from northern and western Europe it was about one-seventh. Among Jews, who composed over one-tenth of the total immigration in this period, the proportion

Table 1.6. Immigrants by occupation at time of entry, 1821–1920.[a]

Period	Total (thousands)	Total reporting occupation (thousands)	Percent reporting occupation	Percent distribution of total reporting occupation				
				Agriculture	Industry and mining	Transport and commerce	Domestic service and general labor	Liberal professions and public service
1821–1830	166	66	39.8	21.4	22.3	36.3	16.8	3.2
1831–1840	640	272	42.6	32.3	27.1	18.5	20.4	1.6
1841–1850	1,703	766	45.0	32.4	21.8	6.7	38.2	0.9
1851–1860	2,940	1,355	46.1	30.5	17.2	10.2	41.5	0.5
1861–1870	2,660	1,241	46.6	17.5	21.0	11.0	49.3	1.2
1871–1880	2,812	1,382	49.1	18.9	21.5	6.6	51.5	1.5
1881–1890	5,247	2,602	49.6	14.5	18.3	5.2	61.0	1.0
1891–1900	3,844	2,147	55.8	11.9	17.4	6.1	63.5	1.0
1901–1910	8,795	6,478	73.6	26.7	17.8	4.7	49.4	1.5
1911–1920	5,736	3,924	68.4	29.8	18.3	6.7	42.5	2.7

Source: Walter F. Willcox, ed., International Migrations, I, Statistics (New York, 1929), pp. 399–400.

a. Figures for 1821–1867 represent alien passengers arriving in steerage; 1868–1891 and 1895–1897, immigrant aliens arriving; 1892–1894 and 1898–1920, immigrant aliens admitted.

reporting an agricultural occupation was only 2.6 percent. It is also possible that some agricultural immigrants who anticipated urban employment may have responded in terms of their prospective urban occupations. Throughout the period of free immigration the highly skilled group in "liberal professions and public services" was a minuscule proportion of the total, averaging less than 2 percent.

A large proportion of immigrants reported no occupation. This group consisted largely of spouses and children, but in the period before 1890 it also included a substantial proportion of persons with "occupation unknown." It is difficult to judge whether omission of the latter group distorts the occupational distribution shown. Except for domestic service, the data for those with occupations refer mainly to male workers.

Immigration restrictions wrought a substantial change in the occupational makeup of immigrants, especially with the establishment after World War II of a system which gave preference to newcomers with special skills. The data on legal immigration show a major shift from an unskilled labor supply to a much more highly skilled one. In the 1960s, for example, the share of professionals had risen to close to one-fourth compared with a mere 1 percent in 1901–1910. In contrast, the share of farm and nonfarm laborers and domestic service workers had dropped to a little over 20 percent from a level exceeding 70 percent in 1901–1910.

Occupations in the United States

The work taken up by U.S. immigrants was even less agricultural than one would have expected from their occupations in their countries of origin. This reflects partly the role of labor demands in the growing American economy in shaping the immigrants' occupational distribution. It is also partly due to the advantages in entering farming that native whites had over immigrants because of greater capital and more pertinent farming experience.

Within the nonagricultural sector, immigrants played a distinctive role in filling the evolving occupational requirements of industrialization. Table 1.7 presents the number of workers in each major occupational group in 1910, the earliest date for which such data are readily available and each group's distribution by color, nativity, and parentage. Although each population group was represented in each occupational class, the native white stock was the predominant group filling white-collar jobs; the foreign stock, manual jobs; and the nonwhite, domestic service. In general, the native white stock predominated in higher-status occupations, the foreign stock occupied an intermediate position, and the nonwhites were at the bottom of the ladder. There is also an interesting difference between the first and second immigrant generations. The children of immigrants had a noticeably larger share than their parents in white-collar occupations and a noticeably lower share in the other, lower-status occupations.

The predominance of the native white stock in the higher-level occupations suggests that this group exerted disproportionate influence in decisions shaping the expansion of urban economic activity in the 19th century. That this is so is dramatically supported by studies of business leaders in the 1870s and from 1900 to 1910. The study for the latter period, for example, covered 190 members of the business elite—men who were either presidents or chairmen of the largest American corporations in manufacturing and mining, railroads, public utilities, and finance, or partners in the leading investment banking houses. In nonfarm occupations as a whole there were only four persons in ten of native white stock, but among the business elite there were eight out of ten. These men (there were no women in the group) were almost all from old American families and of British descent. The largest proportion came from the New England and Middle Atlantic states, and they had business family backgrounds. The poor 19th-century immigrant or poor farm boy who rose "from rags to riches" was a rare exception—only

Table 1.7. Distribution of U.S. labor force in major occupational groups by color, place of birth, and parentage, 1910.

Occupational group	Number (millions)	Distribution by percentage			
		Native whites of native parentage	Native-born whites of foreign or mixed parentage	Foreign-born whites	Nonwhite
Farm	11.5	61	12	9	18
Nonfarm	25.8	42	22	26	10
White Collar	8.0	56	27	17	1
Manual					
Craftsmen and operatives	9.8	40	24	30	6
Laborers	4.5	33	14	37	17
Service workers					
Private household workers	1.9	23	13	21	43
Others	1.7	35	19	26	20
All occupations	37.3	48	19	21	12

Source: D.L. Kaplan and M.C. Casey, *Occupational Trends in the United States, 1900 to 1950* (Washington, D.C., 1958); E.P. Hutchinson, *Immigrants and Their Children, 1850–1950* (New York, 1956).

six people in the entire group fit this description. Thus, the descendants of the colonial white stock played a leading role not only in agricultural settlement but also in decisions shaping urban development. Although the foreign stock were the majority in urban areas, they typically filled the manual occupations necessary for industrial growth. However, the 1910 distribution by occupation of second-generation whites is strikingly like that for those of native parentage. Although the rags-to-riches story is a gross exaggeration, significant economic improvement was possible for those of foreign origin, but the process typically required one generation or more.

Causes of Immigration

Migration between different areas depends on many factors: differences in lifetime earning potentials; the costs of moving; nonmonetary factors such as language, religion, and political conditions; and the extent to which potential migrants possess relevant information. Although all these factors at one time or another affected the flow of persons to the United States, the most persistent and dominant force, especially in the great movements during the period of free immigration, was economic. Various types of data—such as comparative wage rates—make clear that in the 19th century economic opportunities in the United States were generally superior to those in Europe. But although this accounts for the direction of the flow of migrants, it is not sufficient to explain the noticeable variations in migration over time and by area of origin. Why is it that starting in the 1830s a pronounced and sustained increase occurred in the movement of Europeans to the United States? Why did this movement take a wavelike form? Why did the origins of the migrants shift increasingly from northern and western Europe to southern and eastern Europe?

Two developments seem primarily responsible for the continuous uptrend in European emigration throughout the

19th century. One was the industrialization process in the United States and the demands that it generated for manual labor in factories and construction work. Although industrial growth was taking place as early as the 1820s and 1830s, it was not until about 1850 that it reached a magnitude involving labor demands of substantial size. Confronted with the cost of native labor, which was being drained away by western agricultural opportunities, employers sought to recruit cheaper foreign labor by publicizing opportunities in the United States and by other means.

The other principal factor in the increased volume of migration was the surge in population growth in Europe associated with the onset of modernization. When population was stable and sons could succeed to their fathers' positions, the inclination to move was low, especially in traditional societies. But under conditions of accelerated population growth, the opportunities available by virtue of the death or retirement of fathers were fewer than the number of individuals seeking them. A growing number of people were forced to seek new opportunities, including opportunities abroad. The population upsurge in 19th-century Europe placed increasing numbers of people in this position and thereby stimulated emigration. Safer means of travel and a decline in overseas transportation costs during the course of the century strengthened this tendency.

Another possible cause of the increase in European emigration was the occurrence of catastrophic events such as famines, wars, revolutions, epidemics, pogroms, and so on. Such events imply a deterioration in both income-earning prospects and the social advantages of the home country. It is doubtful that catastrophic events explain the continuous rise in emigration, because they occurred before as well as after that rise. But they did help determine which European countries responded most vigorously to opportunities in the United States, a point to be discussed below. And the overall volume of European emigration would have been less if there had been no such dislocations.

The 15–20-year swings in U.S. immigration appear to be due to major surges and declines in American economic conditions and thus in the growth of the demand for labor. A major economic boom or relapse tended to generate a corresponding movement in the flow of people from all the European countries. A tight American labor market offered the prospect of jobs at relatively attractive wage rates; a slack labor market meant great uncertainty about obtaining employment, whatever the wage rate.

Although conditions in the United States were chiefly responsible for immigration fluctuations over time, conditions in Europe were responsible for the distribution in the national origins of the arrivals. Given favorable conditions of labor demand in the United States, the countries that experienced more intense population pressure or catastrophic events typically responded most sensitively to that demand. The Irish exodus during the mid-19th-century potato famine is a case in point. Similarly, the shift in emigration from northern and western to southern and eastern Europe appears to be due to the shifting incidence of modern economic development with its attendant surge in population growth and associated dislocations. This process started in northern and western Europe and proceeded across the face of the continent in the course of the 19th century. Toward the end of the century, as population pressure grew in southern and eastern Europe, this area's overseas emigration rose correspondingly.

The continuing growth of European migration to the United States probably would have resumed after World War I, but it was forestalled by a change in U.S. policy.

Effect of Immigration on Rate of Population Growth

It would seem to be obvious that the free immigration to the United States increased total population growth. It has been argued, however, that immigration may merely have taken the place of native population growth which would otherwise have occurred. Some writers have asserted that the competition of immigrants exerted a negative effect on the fertility of the native population—that in the absence of immigration, native fertility would have been higher and population growth the same. The first president of the American Economic Association, Francis Amasa Walker, argued vigorously in an article entitled "Immigration and Degradation" that "the access of foreigners . . . constituted a shock to the principle of population among the native element" and "as the foreigners began to come in larger numbers, the native population more and more withheld their own increase." In Walker's view, "The American shrank from the industrial competition thus thrust upon him. He was unwilling himself to engage in the lowest kind of day labor with these new elements of the population; he was even more unwilling to bring sons and daughters into the world to enter into that competition."

The argument that immigration led to lower fertility is suspect because declines in American fertility are observed not only in times and places of high immigration but also in circumstances of little or no immigrant competition. Fertility became lower early in the 19th century, even before any substantial influx of immigrants occurred. Moreover, fertility declined not only in the areas of immigrant concentration but in others as well, notably the South. Fertility declines commonly set in in those areas where the land supply had been largely exhausted and the process of settlement completed, not as the result of competition from immigrants.

One must also consider the type of economic activity that the native population would have followed in the absence of immigration. It seems likely that in such circumstances the workers for American industrial expansion would have been drawn more from rural areas than was actually the case. This implies that over time, the native-born population would have been less involved in new settlement and more engaged in urban activities—that is, more exposed to an environment that encouraged low rather than high fertility. If there had been no immigration, then, fertility among the native stock might have been even lower than it was.

It is possible that the mortality of the native population might have been lower in the absence of immigration. It has been argued that immigrants sometimes transmitted epidemic or other contagious diseases to the native population. The evidence suggests a higher life expectancy for native-born than for foreign-born whites: at the beginning of the 20th century, the native-born at age 20 had an edge of about 2.5 years. (The advantage of whites over nonwhites at that time was about 7 years.) By 1940 the differential between the native- and foreign-born white populations had virtually disappeared.

Thus, it is likely that in the absence of immigration both the fertility and mortality of the native white population might have been lower. Taking account of this one can make a rough estimate of the quantitative impact of immigration between 1790 and 1920 on the size of the population. If, in the absence of immigration, natural increase (the excess of fertility over mortality) of the colonial stock would have been the same as it was in the presence of immigration, then between 1790 and 1920 immigrants and their descendants contributed just as much to population growth as did the multiplication of the original colonial stock, white and nonwhite combined. In other words, the actual 1920 population was double that which would have resulted from increase of the colonial stock alone. By region, however, there were important variations. Little of the postcolonial immigration went to the South, and even in 1920 the population of this area was composed very largely of descendants of the colonial population.

Effect of Immigration on Production Growth

What about the effect of immigration on the rate of growth of gross national product (GNP)? In considering this, a distinction between aggregate and per capita GNP is important. With regard to total GNP the effect of immigration is clear. If immigration had been substantially less, the growth of the labor force would have been less rapid and land would have come under cultivation more slowly. With fewer savers, capital accumulation would have been less. The slower growth of land, labor, and capital would in turn have implied a slower growth in aggregate output. Actual trends in the United States over the last century or so are roughly consonant with this reasoning: a continuous decline in the growth rate of population has been accompanied by a continuous decline in the growth rate of national product.

It is when one considers per capita output that the problem becomes most challenging. Between 1790 and 1840 immigration remained low, though it was rising. In the late 1840s, however, a major influx began which, if one includes descendants as well as immigrants, doubled the American population by 1920. Suppose that population growth had been kept much lower by curtailment of immigration. What then would have been the course of per capita output? Would the United States have reached a material standard of living comparable to that which it enjoys today? Or, as some argue, was immigration critically important to rapid growth in material well-being?

There are several ways in which immigration affected growth of per capita output. Immigration altered the age distribution of the population by raising the proportion of the working-age population to total population, and within the working-age population, by keeping the proportion aged 20 to 29 higher than it would otherwise have been. In terms of the effect on per capita product, both influences are favorable—the first because it raises the proportion of workers to dependents and the second because it increases the proportion of more vigorous, younger workers within the working group. However, the quantitative effect on the per capita output is small.

Offsetting these positive influences is the effect of immigration on the general health and educational levels of the labor force. Because the foreign-born had somewhat higher illiteracy rates and lower life expectancy than the native-born, in the absence of immigration the average health and education of the labor force would have shown more rapid improvement, and this would have made for somewhat faster growth in per capita production.

Did immigration add special skills or entrepreneurial abilities to the labor force? Certainly there were immigrants who succeeded as entrepreneurs and others who had special labor skills. The foreign-born, however, are underrepresented among the industrial leaders of the 19th century; the mass of immigrants filled manual jobs, and these could have been done by native workers.

What about economic motivation? Did immigration after 1790 provide a population group with an exceptional urge to get ahead? This seems dubious. A strong interest in material gain runs back to the earliest period of settlement. It was manifest in both towns and rural areas in the 17th century and was the despair of some early religious leaders. The story of land speculation seems much the same whether one is looking at Puritans in 17th-century New England or at their descendants in the 19th-century Midwest.

The principal impetus for rapid economic growth came from the burgeoning developments in modern technology that date from the Industrial Revolution in England toward the end of the 18th century. In the first half-century after 1790, a period in which U.S. immigration was relatively slight, the growth rate of per capita production in the United States rose to levels comparable to those of today, and the American system of manufacturing came into being, a system so distinctive that the world's leading industrial nation, Great Britain, sent a special commission in 1850 to study it. Thus, even before immigration rose markedly in the 19th century, the United States was well started on the transformation of its economy to modern technology.

It is important to note also that in Europe, and especially northwestern Europe, high emigration did not prevent the development of this new technology. In the United States between 1840 and 1957, the shift to modern technology led to a 460 percent increase in real per capita production. In the major European countries real per capita output grew as follows: United Kingdom, 1850s–1950s, 370 percent; West Germany, 1870s–1960s, 520 percent; France, 1840s–1960s, 520 percent. If U.S. growth in per capita production had been especially favored by immigration, the European countries of emigration should have been correspondingly disfavored; but there is little in the figures above to suggest that this was the case.

It seems reasonable to conclude, therefore, that while 19th-century immigration had a major impact on America's size—in terms of both total population and total output—it probably did not alter substantially the growth of output per capita. The major impetuses to the growth of per capita production were rapid innovation through the adoption of modern technology and an associated capital formation. These developments were fostered by a young, vigorous, relatively well-educated population with strong economic motivation operating under institutions which favored the pursuit of personal gain. All these conditions existed prior to the vast 19th-century immigration, and would have continued to operate even in the absence of that immigration.

A Smaller America?

In other respects, however, 19th-century U.S. immigration was of considerable importance. Although per capita product growth might not have been much different in its absence, the economy would have grown much less in aggregate size. In addition, although many of the structural changes in the economy would still have occurred—for example, the proportion of urban concentration, the change in occupational structure, and the shifts in overall consumption patterns—there would have been differences in industrial structure, related in part to greater involvement in world trade. As for geographic expansion, it seems likely that some areas now being depopulated might never have been settled, and the reduction of the indigenous Indian population might not have been so drastic. Without 19th-century immigration, the American population would exhibit much less cultural variety than it does today. Conceivably, the role of women and of nonwhites would have been different. Economic assimilation of nonwhites might have proceeded more rapidly and problems of racial integration might have been posed and resolved sooner. Internationally, a smaller United States more dependent on world trade would have been a less important voice in world politics.

2

SETTLEMENT PATTERNS AND SPATIAL DISTRIBUTION

The complex migrations of American Indians, Europeans, Africans, Asians, and Latin Americans to North America and their subsequent internal migrations have created striking differences in the spatial distribution, or geographic placement, of the various ethnic groups in the United States. Differences in economic advancement, social life, and political preferences among these groups are a recognized fact of American life and have become major preoccupations of public policies. That ethnic groups also exhibit distinctive locational patterns and that their uneven geographic distribution has helped perpetuate regionalism in the United States is less well understood.

Too often the social problems of particular ethnic groups have been related in a simplistic fashion to their segregated residential patterns. Not all segregation, however, is the involuntary consequence of poverty and prejudice. Many ethnic groups cluster in well-defined neighborhoods in an attempt to preserve their identity and community, and such voluntary segregation is not necessarily associated with material deprivation. Problems of ethnic unemployment may be an integral part of regional economic stagnation, but this predicament is caused not only by overrepresentation or segregation of a group but also by the depressed nature of the locale. School desegregation policies explicitly rely upon manipulations of the geographic boundaries of school districts, because such adjustments permit radical alterations in the ethnic composition of the student body. Although these measures certainly confront the problems of segregation, they may also obscure a more basic and persistent geographic element in the residential patterns of deprived ethnic groups: the fact that they live in those parts of the city defined by the poverty of their residents. The relationships between the identity and well-being of ethnic groups and their varied territorial arrangements are so complex that they require consideration at several levels: first, on the large or regional scale; second, on the intermediate or urban scale; and third, on the small or neighborhood scale.

Ethnicity and Geographic Placement

Few ethnic groups are evenly distributed throughout all regions of the United States; the tendency to concentrate in some areas and to avoid others reveals the close relation between ethnicity and territory. Of all the bases upon which human society is differentiated, ethnicity is perhaps the most sensitive to the relations between a group's identity and its past or present geographic placement. Ethnicity, like socioeconomic measures of class or status, defines human groups on the basis of specified traits, but unlike those measures, it groups people according to a common ancestry based upon a shared original homeland. Some ethnic identifications are explicitly locational and refer to a region, province, or nation, although ethnic groups may also be defined by dominant religion, language, or culture associated with the ancestral homeland.

Although complex migrations have radically altered the distribution of many ethnic groups, a group often keeps its ancestral locational identification for generations in a new homeland. In time, some of the ancestral identifications disappear, and at the same time the culture of a group may become so closely associated with its adopted location that during subsequent moves its ethnicity will be defined by reference to the most recent place of residence rather than to the original homeland. For example, English immigrants to New England and the southern colonies developed distinctive provincial subcultures. When these groups moved westward they were identified as New Englanders or Southerners rather than as English Americans. Similarly, French colonists to Quebec and Acadia (Nova Scotia) retained their North American labels in their subsequent movements to New England and Louisiana, respectively. The Mormons, an ethnic group originally defined by a set of religious beliefs, were formed in upstate New York, but today they are most closely identified with their adopted state, Utah. Other groups that have retained their original ethnic identification have become associated with the particular areas of the United States where they are concentrated, for example, the Japanese on the West Coast, Cubans in southern Florida, and Norwegians in the Northern Midwest. Even though many members of such groups live far removed from the region of greatest concentration, their ethnic identity continues to be associated with these regions.

The close relationship between ethnicity and place exists not only regionally but also in the larger cities of the United States. The Chinese and Jews, in particular, have settled in diversified metropolitan cities, and the various Slavic groups have gravitated to several large industrial cities. Because migration over the past century and a half has been largely a cityward movement, the presence of many different groups in one area is most evident in large cities. In spite of this pluralism, residential segregation and institutional differences have helped to maintain distinctive ethnic identities. "Chinatown" most graphically exemplifies the association of a group with a particular part of a city. Although such ethnic quarters are seldom occupied by only one group and usually do not house a majority of the dominant group, most large cities contain a mosaic of districts associated with particular ethnic populations.

Geographic concentration, however, is not a valid criterion for evaluating the social and economic conditions of ethnic groups, and the relationship between residential patterns and socioeconomic status must be evaluated with care. For some groups, concentration in particular regions or in urban neighborhoods is a source of local political power, a basis of economic advancement, and protection for ethnic distinctiveness. On the other hand, concentration may reflect a group's exclusion from full participation in the surrounding society and may therefore be a measure of relative deprivation. This paradox accounts in part for the ambiguity of the term "ghetto," which evocatively captures the synthesis of group identity and spatial concentration. Traditionally used to refer to the legally prescribed Jewish quarter of medieval cities, the word today often denotes the segregated quarters of any ethnic group. Hence, while concentration in a ghetto may imply an adverse and deprived material environment that obstructs economic advancement, it may also suggest a place with distinctive ethnic institutions that reinforce group solidarity and facilitate social well-being. Far more important to the socioeconomic position of an ethnic group than the degree to which it is segregated is its specific location within a city or region, for example, a dilapidated section of the inner city or a region with high unemployment. Moreover, segregated residential patterns are but one geographic aspect of ethnic distribution, because substantial proportions of most American ethnic groups live outside their ghetto or area of greatest concentration.

Ethnic Composition of the Population

The discussion thus far has assumed that American ethnic groups are well defined and that regional and urban concentrations are readily identifiable. On the contrary, not only are data on ethnic groups limited and inconsistent, but rarely are these data presented for appropriate spatial units. Despite its many limitations, the 1970 Census is the most useful source from which to determine the present spatial distribution of American ethnic groups. Except for the fact that larger sections of the South are becoming destinations rather than sources of migrants, there is no evidence of major shifts in the distribution and composition of American ethnic groups since 1970.

In 1970 blacks accounted for 11.1 percent of the total population of the United States; people of Spanish heritage, 4.5 percent; people of Asian descent, 1.0 percent; American Indians, 0.4 percent; and people of European descent, 82.0 percent. The remaining 1.0 percent are grouped in a miscellaneous "other" category. The census also indicates the proportions of these ethnic groupings that were of "foreign stock," a classification that includes both first-generation immigrants (those born in a foreign country) and the second generation (those born in the United States of foreign or mixed parentage). Whereas 80 percent of the Asians and almost 38 percent of the people of Spanish heritage were of foreign stock, only 2 percent of the black population and a little more than 15 percent of the people of European origin fell into that classification.

Unfortunately it is not possible to break down accurately into its ethnic components the 85 percent of Americans of European descent but American-born parentage—to determine, for example, how many Scots or Swedes there are of the third or later generations. According to a 1971 Census Bureau inquiry, however, almost one-half of the people of European heritage who were questioned about their ancestry claimed one of the following seven national origins: English, Scottish, or Welsh (15.3 percent); German (12.6 percent); Irish (8.0 percent); Italian (4.3 percent); French (2.6 percent); Polish (2.4 percent); and Russian (1.1 percent). Had the list of origins been more inclusive, more people might have declared a specific ancestry. Although these responses do not necessarily indicate a well-defined ethnic identity, they do show that many Americans of European descent but American parentage are aware of their national origins.

National origins are not appropriate ethnic indicators for all groups. Religious affiliation is clearly a more sensitive measure for Jews, Mormons, and many smaller sectarian groups, such as the Mennonites. Unfortunately, statistical data on congregational membership are unreliable, but they do tend to confirm the impression of uneven distribution of religious groups. Ancestral language also remains a definitive trait for most foreign-born immigrants, of whom only about 18 percent claim English as their mother tongue (the language spoken in the home when they were children). In the absence of continued immigration of an ethnic group, the persistence of the mother tongue after prolonged residence in the United States is quite rare: 82 percent of the American-born population claim English as their mother tongue. In most groups, persistence of the ancestral tongue is confined to a small minority.

Regional Patterns

If the United States is divided into 12 regions, the geographic patterns of the major ethnic groups are very distinctive. This divisional scheme is a slight modification of the Census Bureau's groupings of states, which often combine regions with strikingly different migration histories into one unit. Specifically, the South Atlantic region has been subdivided into the Upper South Atlantic and the Southeast to distinguish those areas that are part of the northeastern metropolitan corridor from the southeastern areas. The eastern and western North Central states have been combined and then divided into three sections that are more consistent with the dominant paths of westward migration: the Eastern Midwest, Northern Midwest, and Southern Midwest. For similar reasons, the Mountain and Pacific regions have been altered to accommodate migratory distinctions between the Southwest and the Northwest.

In 1970 the most striking spatial patterns were those of some ethnic groups that were confined to extremely small areas of the United States. More than three-quarters of the population of Puerto Rican heritage were concentrated in the Mid-Atlantic states, primarily in the New York City area. Almost one-half of the population of Cuban origin were clustered in the Southeast, especially in and around Miami, and most of the other half were in the New York area. About one-half of the population of Mexican origin resided in California and the Southwest, and most of the remaining half lived in the adjacent West South Central region. These two adjacent regions also contained about one-half of the American Indian population; most of the other half were widely dispersed throughout all the western states. About one-third of both the Japanese and the Chinese were concentrated in California, but a second and equally large group of Chinese was clustered in the Mid-Atlantic region, and a large group of Japanese lived in Hawaii.

Similar patterns of concentration were visible among groups of European origin. In 1970 several first- and second-generation European ethnic groups were very heavily concentrated in New England, the Mid-Atlantic states, and the Eastern Midwest. Two-thirds of the first- and second-generation Irish and Italians lived in New England and the Mid-Atlantic states. Russians (mainly but not entirely Jewish) were also highly concentrated in the Northeast; almost 70 percent resided in the Mid-Atlantic states, primarily in the metropolitan areas of New York and Philadelphia. Two-thirds of the first and second generations of Poles, Czechs, Hungarians, and Yugoslavs, and more than half of the Greeks lived in the Mid-Atlantic and Eastern Midwest regions. The groups from northwestern Europe, particularly the Scandinavians, were more dispersed, but substantial proportions were concentrated in the Midwest and Pacific Northwest. The Southeast and the two South Central regions contained few people of foreign stock; they were populated mainly by blacks and whites of American parentage. These three southern regions, which in 1970 included about one-quarter of the total population of the United States, contained almost one-half of the black population. Most of the remainder lived in the Mid-Atlantic states and the Eastern Midwest. More than one-quarter of the French-speaking population resided in the Western South Central states, and more than one-third in New England. French Canadians from Quebec were concentrated in New England and the adjacent portions of New York, and almost all those of Acadian descent were in Louisiana.

Comparison of the proportion of each group living in a given region with the proportion of the total population living in that region reveals further spatial distinctions. Tables 2.1 and 2.2 indicate that the common practice of aggregating individual ethnic groups into larger units, such as the Spanish-speaking, the Slavs, or the Scandinavians, tends to obscure the spatial patterns of each constituent group. For example, the differences among the geographical patterns of the three major ethnic components of the Spanish-speaking group (Mexicans, Cubans, and Puerto Ricans) are far greater than the differences between these groups and many non-Spanish-speaking populations. As Table 2.1 shows, the one common element in the geographical patterns of all three Spanish-speaking components was their high level of overrepresentation in three distinct regions: the Mexicans in the Southwest, the Cubans in Florida, and the Puerto Ricans in New York. Asians were quite highly overrepresented in California and also to some extent in the Pacific Northwest. Japanese Americans were slightly overrepresented in the Mountain region but not in any of the southern, midwestern, or northeastern regions. The Chinese were underrepresented in all four of these areas but overrepresented in the Mid-Atlantic states. Like both the Mexicans and the Asians, American Indians were strikingly overrepresented in California and the Southwest, but they were also overrepre-

Table 2.1. Relative regional representation of non-European ethnic groups, 1970.[a]

Region	American Indian	Black	Mexican	Cuban	Puerto Rican	Chinese	Japanese
New England	0.2	0.3	*	0.4	0.8	0.7	0.2
Mid-Atlantic	0.3	1.0	*	1.6	4.2	1.2	0.3
Eastern Midwest	0.3	0.9	0.4	0.3	0.5	0.4	0.3
Northern Midwest	2.4	*	*	*	*	0.3	0.2
Southern Midwest	0.2	0.5	0.2	0.1	*	*	0.2
Upper South Atlantic	0.2	1.7	*	0.3	0.2	0.5	0.2
Southeast	0.8	2.0	*	5.0	0.3	0.1	0.2
Eastern South Central	0.2	1.8	*	0.1	0.1	0.2	0.1
Western South Central	1.6	1.4	3.8	0.3	0.1	0.3	0.2
California, Southwest	3.0	0.6	4.5	0.8	0.3	3.7	3.3
Mountain	3.1	*	1.2	*	*	0.4	1.1
Pacific Northwest	2.2	*	0.4	*	*	1.2	1.7

Source: U.S. Bureau of the Census, *Census of the Population, 1970,* vol. 1, *Characteristics of the Population,* pt. 1, *U.S. Summary* (Washington, D.C., 1973), I, p. 293, table 60; U.S. Bureau of the Census, *Census of the Population, 1970,* Subject Report PC(2)-1C, *Persons of Spanish Origin* (Washington, D.C., 1973), pp. 2–4, table 1.

a. The value of 1.0 indicates that the proportion of an ethnic group living in a given region equaled the proportion of the total national population living in that region. Values below 1.0 indicate underrepresentation, and values above 1.0 indicate overrepresentation.

* Values less than 0.1.

Table 2.2. Relative regional representation of European ethnic groups by country or origin, 1970.[a]

Country of origin	New England	Mid-Atlantic	Eastern Midwest	Northern Midwest	Southern Midwest
United Kingdom	2.0	1.6	0.9	0.6	0.5
Ireland	3.8	2.4	0.7	0.4	0.4
Germany	0.7	1.4	1.2	2.5	1.4
Norway	0.5	0.6	0.5	7.7	0.8
Sweden	1.6	0.6	1.1	4.2	1.2
Denmark	0.7	0.6	0.7	3.4	2.2
Netherlands	0.5	0.9	1.7	1.9	1.2
France	0.4	1.6	0.8	0.6	0.7
Switzerland	0.8	1.1	0.9	1.9	1.2
Austria	0.8	2.6	1.0	1.0	0.5
Hungary	0.8	2.2	1.6	0.6	0.3
Poland	1.8	2.3	1.6	0.9	0.2
U.S.S.R.	1.5	2.4	0.7	1.0	0.5
Czechoslovakia	0.6	1.9	1.7	1.4	1.0
Yugoslavia	0.2	1.4	2.3	1.6	0.6
Italy	2.5	3.0	0.7	0.2	0.2
Greece	2.4	1.8	1.3	0.4	0.3
Canada	5.3	0.7	1.0	0.8	0.3
French mother tongue[b]	6.0	0.6	0.4	0.5	0.2

Source: U.S. Bureau of the Census, *Census of the Population, 1970*, vol. 1, *Characteristics of the Population*, pt. 1, *U.S. Summary* (Washington, D.C., 1973), I, pp. 473–480, tables 144–147.

a. The value of 1.0 indicates that the proportion of an ethnic group living in a given region equaled the proportion of the total national population living in

sented in the Mountain region, the Pacific Northwest, the Northern Midwest, and to a lesser degree, in the Western South Central states. Blacks were overrepresented only in the four southern regions; their representation in the Mid-Atlantic and Eastern Midwest was approximately the same as in the nation as a whole.

Table 2.2 shows that although most European groups were

Table 2.2. *(Continued)*

Upper South Atlantic	Southeast	Eastern South Central	Western South Central	California– Southwest	Mountain	Pacific Northwest
0.7	0.6	0.2	0.3	1.5	1.3	1.3
0.5	0.3	0.1	0.1	0.7	0.5	0.5
0.5	0.5	0.2	0.4	1.0	1.0	1.1
0.2	0.3	0.1	0.1	1.1	1.8	4.7
0.2	0.4	0.1	0.2	1.3	1.7	2.9
0.3	0.4	0.1	0.2	1.8	3.0	2.6
0.3	0.4	0.1	0.2	1.7	1.6	1.7
0.8	0.6	0.3	0.5	1.8	1.0	1.0
0.5	0.4	0.2	0.3	2.0	1.8	2.4
0.5	0.4	0.1	0.2	0.8	0.7	0.6
0.5	0.5	0.1	0.1	0.9	0.3	0.4
0.5	0.3	0.1	0.1	0.5	0.2	0.2
0.6	0.5	0.1	0.1	1.1	0.7	0.7
0.5	0.3	0.1	0.5	0.6	0.5	0.5
0.3	0.2	0.1	0.1	1.2	1.1	0.9
0.4	0.2	0.1	0.2	0.8	0.4	0.3
0.9	0.5	0.2	0.2	1.0	0.8	0.6
0.4	0.5	0.3	0.2	1.4	0.9	2.3
0.4	0.3	0.2	2.7	0.8	0.4	0.5

that region. Values below 1.0 indicate underrepresentation, and values above 1.0 indicate overrepresentation.

b. Primarily people of Quebec origin living in New England and those of Acadian origin living in Louisiana.

overrepresented in the New England, Mid-Atlantic, and Midwest regions, the parameters for these ethnic groups varied considerably. Again the practice of grouping has obscured the regional distribution of each component group. Among the first- and second-generation Scandinavians, for instance, only the Swedes were overrepresented in New England and well represented throughout the Midwest; the

Norwegians were highly overrepresented in the northern sections of the Midwest but underrepresented in the eastern and southern parts. Of Slavic Americans, only Poles were overrepresented in New England; in fact, their regional distribution was closer to that of the Greeks than to that of other Slavic groups. If, however, first- and second-generation Europeans are divided into four large groupings—those from northwestern Europe, those from Ireland, the Slavs, and those from Mediterranean countries—the most striking regional pattern evident in 1970 was the overrepresentation of northwestern Europeans in the three western regions of the United States. Especially prominent were the Norwegians in the Pacific Northwest and the Danes in the Mountain states. By contrast, the Irish, the Slavs (with the exception of the Yugoslavs), and people from the Mediterranean countries were underrepresented in these regions. The regional distribution of later generations of each ethnic group—the descendants of 19th-century immigrants—was probably very similar to that of the first and second generations. The geographical distributions of both first and second generations in 1970 certainly approximated the historic regional concentrations of earlier immigrants of the same ethnic group, whose patterns will be discussed later.

Urban Concentrations

Ethnic groups are also differentiated by their varying levels of concentration in cities. In 1970 some 73 percent of the total U.S. population lived in settlements of 2,500 inhabitants or more, and 58 percent resided in places, usually of more than 50,000 people, that are subdivided in the census into central city and fringe (largely suburban) areas. The residents of all the central cities together accounted for about 31 percent of the population and those of the urban fringes for about 27 percent. Of the remaining 42 percent of the total population, about 15 percent lived in towns and about 27 percent in rural areas (settlements smaller than 2,500). Approximately half of the inhabitants of small urban centers lived in places of about 10,000 to 50,000 people, the other half in places with populations between 2,500 and 10,000. The remaining 27 percent of the population were classified as rural, but only 4 percent of the total were described as "rural farm." Because the vast majority of the total American population lived in cities and towns, and more than half lived in large cities, the varying levels of urban concentration among ethnic groups were less striking than their locations within the cities.

The distinction between central city and urban fringe is useful, even though central city does not always refer to the deprived inner-city slums, and urban fringe does not necessarily imply desirable living conditions. The proportionate representations of different ethnic groups in the central cities and urban fringes varied considerably in 1970. No less than 83 percent of Puerto Rican Americans were concentrated in the central cities, compared to 60 percent of the blacks and more than 50 percent of those of Hispanic and Asian origin. In contrast, 38 percent of first- and second-generation Europeans and 24 percent of later-generation Europeans lived in the central cities. The proportions of these latter two groups in the urban fringes were 37 and 28 percent, respectively. Thus one-quarter of first- and second-generation Americans of European origin lived in small towns and rural areas, and almost half of the later generations lived there.

Striking differences existed, however, among the individual ethnic groups of European, Spanish, and Asian heritage and also between the first and second generations of each group. Because the movement of groups from the central city to the urban fringe is often related to material advancement, differences in urban residential patterns between the first and second generations of several groups ought to reveal the selective nature of this process. Table 2.3 shows urban concentrations of the first and second generations of each group in 1970. More than 70 percent of first-generation Chinese and approximately 60 percent of first-generation immigrants

Table 2.3. Percentages of ethnic groups in central cities and urban fringes by country of origin and generation, 1970.

	First generation		Second generation	
Country of origin	Central cities	Urban fringes	Central cities	Urban fringes
United Kingdom	35.2	43.1	29.4	40.4
Ireland	58.2	31.9	43.0	40.0
Germany	40.1	36.1	30.8	31.5
Norway	38.0	27.8	26.9	23.4
Sweden	38.6	31.5	29.6	30.0
Denmark	32.8	34.4	26.8	28.8
Netherlands	30.0	40.1	24.2	34.6
France	44.8	35.7	33.9	36.8
Switzerland	33.4	36.6	27.2	30.1
Austria	51.4	31.5	37.7	40.0
Hungary	50.3	35.9	36.2	44.5
U.S.S.R.	61.1	28.3	46.5	38.2
Poland	60.4	28.6	43.5	39.0
Czechoslovakia	42.9	36.0	29.4	39.4
Yugoslavia	52.9	33.1	34.1	42.0
Italy	51.9	36.5	40.2	43.8
Greece	62.4	28.1	44.0	40.5
Canada	32.8	40.0	27.8	36.6
French mother tongue[a]	43.9	31.7	29.9[b]	24.5[b]
Cuba	57.7	39.0	52.0	39.2
Mexico	50.4	32.8	46.1	24.1
China	71.5	19.2	61.1	25.7
Japan	50.0	27.3	44.5	28.5

Source: U.S. Bureau of the Census, *Census of the Population, 1970,* vol. I, *Characteristics of the Population,* pt. 1, *U.S. Summary* (Washington, D.C., 1973), I, 103, table 97.

a. Primarily people of Quebec origin living in New England and those of Acadian origin living in Louisiana.

b. Applies to those of American-born parentage.

from Greece, Russia, Poland, Ireland, and Cuba were clustered in the urban centers. Although half or less than half of the first-generation migrants from all other countries lived in central cities, their proportions on the urban fringes were even lower, with the exception of immigrants from Canada, the United Kingdom, Denmark, Holland, and Switzerland. These ethnic differences among the first generation were roughly paralleled among their children. In the second generation, however, the dominance of the central city over the fringe was either reduced or eliminated. Again the same groups showed the largest percentages living in the central cities, but the percentages were decidedly lower. Among Czechs, Yugoslavs, and northwestern Europeans, higher proportions lived on the urban fringes than in the central cities. Indeed, the second generation of all ethnic groups from northwestern Europe, with the exception of Norwegians, were represented in higher proportions on the urban fringes than was the population as a whole. Only one-half of the Norwegians, however, lived in urban areas. Overall about 27 percent of the total population lived on the urban fringes, compared to 30 to 40 percent of second-generation northwestern Europeans.

Representations of ethnic groups in small towns and rural areas also showed a good deal of variation, as Table 2.4 indicates. French Canadians, who predominated in New England and Louisiana, had the highest levels of representation in both towns and rural areas. Later-generation French-speaking Americans had the highest proportion (19 percent) of any group in towns—even higher than that of the population as a whole (15 percent), and they were represented in rural areas in the same proportion as the total population (27 percent). Other groups that were proportionately overrepresented in small towns and rural areas were second-generation Norwegians, Danish, Dutch, and Swiss; Swedes were represented in about the same proportions as was the population as a whole (42 percent). Of the groups underrepresented in towns and rural areas, Germans, Czechs, Yugo-

Table 2.4. Percentages of ethnic groups in small towns and rural areas, by country of origin and generation, 1970.

Country of origin	First generation			Second generation		
	Towns over 10,000	Towns 2,500 to 10,000	Rural areas (under 2,500)	Towns over 10,000	Towns 2,500 to 10,000	Rural areas
United Kingdom	5.0	4.4	12.2	6.6	6.0	17.6
Ireland	2.4	2.0	5.6	4.1	3.4	9.5
Germany	5.1	4.4	14.2	7.4	6.6	23.7
Norway	6.5	5.7	21.4	8.7	8.3	32.7
Sweden	6.5	5.6	17.7	8.1	7.5	24.9
Denmark	6.1	7.1	20.1	8.2	8.0	28.3
Netherlands	5.0	5.5	19.5	6.3	6.8	28.2
France	4.9	4.1	10.7	6.8	5.7	16.8
Switzerland	5.4	4.9	19.5	7.4	7.6	27.8
Austria	3.4	3.4	10.1	4.2	4.2	13.9
Hungary	2.7	2.1	8.9	3.3	3.0	12.9
U.S.S.R.	2.9	1.8	5.9	3.8	2.3	9.1
Poland	2.5	1.9	6.5	3.6	3.0	11.0
Czechoslovakia	3.2	3.9	13.7	4.9	5.8	20.5
Yugoslavia	3.0	2.6	8.8	4.9	4.4	14.3
Italy	3.6	2.6	5.3	4.2	3.4	8.4
Greece	4.0	2.2	3.4	4.9	3.0	7.4
Canada	6.9	5.3	14.9	8.2	6.6	20.8
French mother tongue	7.0	5.0	12.3	10.6[a]	8.7[a]	26.2[a]
Cuba	1.5	0.7	1.1	3.2	1.6	4.0
Mexico	6.7	6.4	12.5	8.0	7.8	13.7
China	4.2	1.6	2.9	5.1	2.5	5.3
Japan	6.6	5.2	10.8	8.4	6.1	12.5

Source: U.S. Bureau of the Census, *Census of the Population, 1970,* vol. I, *Characteristics of the Population,* pt. 1, *U.S. Summary* (Washington, D.C., 1973). I, 103, table 97.
  a. Applies to those of American-born parentage.

slavs, Japanese, and Mexicans, as well as blacks (with 30 percent) were better represented than were Italians, Greeks, Russians, and Cubans.

These noticeable ethnic differences in settlement resulted to some degree from the patterns of regional concentration, for the urban proportions of the population varied considerably from region to region. Groups concentrated in the Mid-Atlantic region, for instance, were far more likely to be living in large cities than groups that had settled in parts of the South. Nevertheless, even in the same region, the various groups differed in their proportionate distribution in central cities, urban fringes, small towns, and rural areas.

Ghetto and Other Small-Scale Patterns

Large-scale regional and urban patterns obscure both the distinctive spatial patterns of many smaller groups and the degree to which different groups are segregated from one another within a larger area. Some of the most extreme examples of concentration are found among small religious groups that seek to maintain their identity and way of life through spatial and social isolation. Although the Mennonites, Hutterites, and other such groups are to some extent concentrated in specific regions, their most distinctive spatial patterns are the high concentration and ethnic exclusiveness of their settlements in any region. High levels of small-scale concentration also occur among rural American Indians both on and off reservations, as well as among rural blacks. Descendants of European immigrants may also be highly segregated. Many settlements in the Midwest are dominated by particular European ethnic groups, such as the extensive concentration of the Dutch in the Kalamazoo, Mich., area or the smaller clusters of Swiss in Wisconsin. Regardless of size, these ethnic concentrations are highly visible because they are unusual: normally, rural ethnic groups are interspersed with at least one or two other groups; they maintain their ethnic identity without depending on either exclusivity or propinquity.

Until recently, the typical urban immigrant experience was considered to be initial concentration in the least desirable sections of the inner city, followed by the second generation's socioeconomic advancement, assimilation, and dispersal to the suburbs. The suburbs, therefore, were presumed to house the assimilated descendants of ethnic migrants. Although observers have acknowledged the variable rates of suburbanization among different groups and also the persistence of ancestral religious loyalties, they have generally accepted the relationship between inner-city segregation and the maintenance of ethnic consciousness, on one hand, and the relationship between suburbanization and assimilation, on the other. Consequently, their efforts to explain the persisting inner-city segregation of blacks and certain other minorities presupposed a sharp contrast between these groups and an ethnically undifferentiated and assimilated suburban population of European origin.

Recent reinterpretations of the urban spatial patterns of European immigrants and their descendants suggest that while some ethnic groups have reconcentrated in suburban locations, others have maintained a strong presence in inner-city neighborhoods. To be sure, a varying proportion of each of these groups has dispersed into areas with no well-defined ethnic identity. Between 1930 and 1960 there was a greater reduction in residential segregation among first- and second-generation Americans of European origin than among blacks and Americans of Spanish heritage, but these reductions were not large. Considerable proportions of all groups lived in census tracts in which they were substantially overrepresented. For example, a recent survey of the New York–Northeastern New Jersey Consolidated Census Area revealed that blacks, Puerto Ricans, and first- and second-generation Europeans were indeed segregated, but that many individual European ethnic groups were just as highly segregated from one another as from blacks and Puerto

Ricans. Norwegians, for example, were one of the most highly localized groups, and although their separation from blacks was especially marked, their separation from Russian Jews was even greater. Moreover, the patterns of segregation did not conform to the expected pattern; the longer-established groups from northwestern Europe were not less segregated than the more recent immigrants from southern and eastern Europe, nor were Protestant groups always more segregated from Catholic groups than from other Protestants. Consequently, earlier assertions that ethnic pluralism would gradually be simplified into religious pluralism, as individual ethnic groups merged into broader, religious-based groupings, are now open to question.

Conditions in the New York–New Jersey area are not necessarily replicated in other cities, but because the issue has been raised, ethnicity must be examined not only in social relations and political behavior but also in residential patterns. The familiar pattern of initial settlement in an inner-city ghetto followed by advancement, assimilation, and relocation in a suburb according to socioeconomic status is but one of many different paths. Although members of the same ethnic group have of course followed different paths, some general observations can be made about the residential patterns of particular groups.

First, the 19th-century northern European immigrants and their descendants did abandon their original locations to later arrivals, and in their new suburban neighborhoods they neglected or even rejected many of their Old World traits. Second, other groups—especially Jewish immigrants and their descendants—have reconcentrated in well-defined suburban sections, and their new, affluent residential quarters, called "gilded ghettos" by one observer, are nearly as closely identified with the ethnicity of their residents as were their original inner-city ghettos. Third, Italians and Slavs have retained sections of their original inner-city quarters and experienced modest rates of suburbanization. Often the population distribution of these groups resembles a wedge, with its base in the inner-city or older suburban neighborhood and its apex in the newer outer suburbs, where representation decreases.

Finally, some ethnic groups, through a combination of poverty and prejudice, have remained heavily concentrated in the least desirable sections of the inner city. Blacks and Spanish-speaking groups belong to this category of involuntary segregation. When the housing supply of these groups is reduced by redevelopment, highway improvement, or simply physical deterioration, they have not always been able to relocate in adjacent areas. Some adjacent areas are occupied by other ethnic groups that are either at the ceiling of their own economic advancement or highly committed to their local ethnic institutions; such groups are unwilling to make room for new groups that attempt to infiltrate their neighborhood. These locational circumstances are often at the root of interethnic tension and conflict.

Not all ethnic groups display patterns of residential concentration. Perhaps the most obvious examples are immigrants from England and English-speaking Canada, who have often gained immediate access to the middle ranks of American society and have quickly merged into the neighborhoods of native-born Americans. Some more visible groups, notably Japanese and Koreans, have maintained a sense of group identity without the base of an ethnic neighborhood. Also, increasing numbers of almost all ethnic groups are far removed from their original quarters. Still, there is no reason to believe that less exclusive and less well-defined residential patterns will necessarily diminish the impact of ethnicity on social interaction or political behavior.

Development of Regional Patterns

The distinctive spatial patterns of American ethnic groups have taken shape over several centuries of immigration and internal migration. Although the ethnic composition of the

American population was already complex by the latter part of the 17th century, both the proportions of the various ethnic groups in the total population and the groups' geographical patterns have changed markedly. The most impressive changes have occurred in response to "push" factors in the countries or regions of origin, which altered the ethnic composition of the immigrant stream to the United States, and "pull" factors in different parts of the United States, which affected the immigrants' choices of destination. Once these combined influences had altered the composition and direction of migration, inertia often set in for a considerable period. The social groupings and information networks established by pioneering migrants influenced the destinations of those who followed, often long after the attraction of a destination had diminished. Thus the spatial differences established during the initial concentrations of each group persisted long after the flow of migration had ceased.

Major changes in the destinations of migrants to and within the United States occurred during the late 18th century, the fourth and eighth decades of the 19th century, and the second decade of the 20th century. Accordingly, the changes in the geography of migration that have most strongly influenced the present distribution of American ethnic groups fit into five historical periods: before 1775, 1775–1850, 1850–1890, 1890–1920, and 1920 to the present.

Before 1775

It is impossible to give an exact picture of the volume and composition of immigration to colonial America, because the available estimates either have been based upon fragmentary sources or have been inferred retrospectively from later data. But we do know that during the colonial period there were several well-defined peaks of immigration, the three highest in the 1720s, the 1740s, and the decade preceding the Revolution (1765–1775). Immigrants from Ulster and the German states dominated during the first two periods, and the Irish, both Protestant and Catholic, were predominant during the final surge. During the same century, immigration accounted for 15 to 20 percent of the growth of the white population, and the international slave trade accounted for 30 to 40 percent of the growth of the black.

The composition of the American population before 1775 must be inferred from data compiled for the first federal census in 1790. At that time, the population was composed of perhaps a half-million American Indians, about one million blacks, and almost four million people of European descent. As Table 2.5 shows, the English and Welsh accounted for about 50 percent of the total (not counting the Indians, whose numbers are quite uncertain) and Scots and Irish for an additional 14 percent. The Germans, the second largest European group, made up 7 percent of the population, but like the immigrants from the British Isles, they were from diverse provincial origins and religious groups. The Dutch, French, and Swedes accounted for most of the remaining population of European heritage.

With an overwhelming majority of the colonists from the British Isles, one might expect the population to have been fairly homogeneous, with little regional variation. On the contrary, the Old World differences within this large group were compounded and differentially altered in the New World. Distinct English subcultures appeared in New England, the Virginia and Maryland tidewater area, and the coastal Carolinas. Some of the differences among English colonists could be attributed to their regional origins, but their most obvious difference was religion. Nonconformists or dissenters, eventually regrouped as Congregationalists, predominated in New England, while Anglicans dominated the coastal South until about 1750. At that time these two denominations had the largest number of churches, but the Presbyterians and Baptists, as well as the German and Dutch ethnic churches, had grown more rapidly in the preceding half-century. Although the Congregationalists maintained their regional dominance into the 19th century, the Anglican

Table 2.5. Percentage of population and relative regional representation of ethnic groups, 1790.

Group	Proportion of total population	Relative regional representation[a]					
		New England	Mid-Atlantic	Delaware	Upper South Atlantic	Southeast	Eastern South Central
English and Welsh	49.2	1.4	0.8	0.9	0.8	0.9	1.0
Scots	6.6	0.6	1.1	0.9	0.9	1.5	1.3
Ulster Irish	4.8	0.7	1.6	1.0	0.8	1.0	1.2
Other Irish	2.9	0.6	1.1	1.5	1.2	1.1	1.5
Germans	7.0	—	2.7	0.1	0.7	0.5	1.7
Dutch	2.5	0.1	3.8	1.3	0.1	0.1	0.4
French	1.4	0.6	1.8	0.9	0.6	1.1	1.3
Swedish	0.5	—	2.2	9.5	0.6	0.3	0.9
Free black	1.5	0.9	1.0	4.4	1.3	0.7	0.6
Slave black	17.8	—	0.2	0.9	2.1	1.8	0.8
Unassigned	5.6						

Source: American Council of Learned Societies, "Report of the Committee on Linguistic and National Stocks in the Population of the United States," *Annual Report of the American Historical Association* 1 (Washington, D.C., 1932), table 13.

a. The value of 1.0 indicates that the proportion of an ethnic group living in a given region equaled the proportion of the total national population living in that region. Values below 1.0 indicate underrepresentation, and values above 1, overrepresentation.

church suffered large defections to the Baptists and Methodists.

Another factor contributing to the emergence or persistence of ethnic identities was the immigrants' uneven regional distribution. When blacks, who constituted about 20 percent of the population (almost twice their present proportion), are included in the computations of the regional representation of ethnic groups as given in Table 2.5, it can be seen that the English and Welsh were overrepresented only in the New England colonies. However, their underrepresentation in the other regions was very slight. Other groups had more striking patterns of concentration. Immigrants from Ulster and the Scots, Germans, Dutch, French, and Swedes were overrepresented in the Mid-Atlantic region, but the Scots were more overrepresented in the Southeast, especially in North Carolina. Table 2.5 devotes a separate column to Delaware, because it was the transitional colony (and later, state) between the Mid-Atlantic and Upper South Atlantic regions. Although the representation of black slaves in Delaware was close to that of the population as a whole and much greater than in the Mid-Atlantic region, it was far less than in the two southern regions. Free blacks, on the other hand, were greatly overrepresented in the Delaware population. Also overrepresented there were several of the non-English European groups that are usually associated with the Mid-Atlantic region, notably the descendants of the early Swedish colony.

In the two southern regions the proportion of blacks was twice as high as it was in the population at large. The non-British groups were greatly underrepresented, except for certain groups such as French Huguenots in South Carolina and German Protestants in North Carolina. The Eastern South Central region had less than 3 percent of the total population of the colonies, primarily in Kentucky and Tennessee; with the exception of the Dutch, the European ethnic groups were well represented there.

About 44,000 people lived in the French and Spanish territories of North America, which are not shown in Table 2.5.

Almost all of the 20,000 persons in the Spanish holdings were of Spanish heritage, but only about 65 percent of the population under French control was of French heritage; the largest minorities were English and Germans. Most of the American Indians on the Atlantic seaboard during the colonial period were displaced by immigrants or ravaged by European epidemic diseases; the pattern of life of those in the interior was altered by the fur trade and related territorial rivalries of Britain, France, Spain, and the colonies themselves.

As the colonial period progressed, ethnic diversity became particularly evident in the Middle (Mid-Atlantic) Colonies and to a more limited degree in the South. Immigration to New England was limited after the Puritan migration of the 1630s. Instead, the greater economic potential and avowed religious toleration of Pennsylvania attracted the majority of new immigrants, who increasingly came from Ulster and the German states. Small-scale farming in the hinterland of Philadelphia appealed to an especially diverse population. Although some of the German pietist groups were highly concentrated, recent research suggests that other ethnic groups were intermixed; the level of ethnic pluralism in the Middle Colonies was unmatched in any of the small nation-states of Europe.

In the South—the tidewater Chesapeake area and coastal South Carolina—the emergence of large-scale plantation agriculture was responsible for the forced immigration of blacks from Africa and the West Indies. Only a minority of white Southerners owned large amounts of land and substantial numbers of slaves; most were small farmers, almost all from the British Isles.

1775–1850

Throughout the Revolutionary and Napoleonic wars, foreign immigration was slight. Although the flow of immigrants resumed in the 1820s, only in the 1840s did it begin to have a significant impact on the ethnic composition of the country.

The period before 1850 was one of considerable internal migration, however. Even before the Revolution, New Englanders moved northward, and Southerners and Middle Colonists had moved southwestward down the Great Valley of Virginia and through the Cumberland Gap into Kentucky and Tennessee. After the Revolution, the Mohawk Valley of upstate New York and the upper reaches of the Ohio River attracted New Englanders and Middle Colonists. New Englanders continued to dominate upstate New York, while the Southerners and Middle Colonists who had moved down the Shenandoah Valley merged with those who had pushed along the upper Ohio to create in the Ohio Valley a diverse population drawn from most of the original colonies. As cotton production expanded, Southerners also moved westward into the Lower Mississippi Valley, and the organization of an internal slave trade caused a corresponding movement of blacks from their original concentrations in the Chesapeake tidewater area and coastal South Carolina to the cotton plantations of Georgia, Alabama, and Mississippi. The extension of the southern plantation system brought to these areas hosts of small farmers who were not slave owners but whose economic fortunes were tied to cotton production and whose social relationships were strongly influenced by the presence of large numbers of black slaves. Other Southerners settled in isolated areas of the Appalachians or Ozarks and maintained only loose connections with the market economy and with the southern and national cultures. Impoverished and isolated, these Southerners formed a distinct ethnic culture and tenaciously maintained the cultural patterns of their English or Scotch-Irish ancestors.

By the time the southern and Ohio Valley frontiers had reached the Mississippi Valley, New England pioneers had moved no farther west than upstate New York. Those who had looked beyond the Niagara River had found Upper Canada (western Ontario) more inviting than northern Ohio. The economic development of the Northern Midwest did not occur until export markets for wheat were developed, just as earlier settlement had been stimulated by the demand for cotton from the South and pork from the Ohio Valley. The Erie Canal, which linked upstate New York with the Atlantic seaboard, did not serve the Midwest until the 1840s, when New Englanders pushed on to the Great Lakes area in response to the improving market for wheat.

In 1820, as Table 2.6 indicates, about 14 percent of the total population of the United States was living in the two South Central regions and less than 9 percent had settled in the Midwest. By 1850 this situation had changed drastically. More than 18 percent lived in the Eastern Midwest alone,

Table 2.6. Regional distribution of the U.S. population, 1790–1970 (in percentages).

	1790	1820	1850	1890	1920	1970
East						
New England	25.8	17.3	11.8	7.4	7.0	5.8
Mid-Atlantic	24.2	28.0	25.4	20.3	21.1	18.3
Midwest						
Eastern	0.2	8.1	18.2	18.9	17.8	17.6
Northern	*	0.1	1.3	5.6	6.0	4.7
Southern	*	0.7	3.8	11.3	8.4	5.5
South						
Upper South Atlantic	28.6	16.4	9.8	6.2	6.0	5.7
Southeast	18.4	15.4	10.9	8.0	7.2	9.4
Eastern South						
Central	2.8	12.4	14.5	10.3	8.4	6.3
West						
Western South						
Central	*	1.7	4.1	7.3	9.7	9.5
California, Southwest	*	*	0.7	2.1	3.9	10.9
Mountain	*	*	*	1.5	2.5	2.7
Pacific Northwest	*	*	*	1.0	2.0	2.7

Source: U.S. Bureau of the Census, *Historical Statistics of the United States* (Washington, D.C., 1961), pp. 12–13.
* Not yet part of the U.S., unsettled, or less than 0.1 percent of population.

Table 2.7. Relative regional representation of Afro-Americans, 1850–1970.[a]

Region	1790	1850	1890	1920	1970
New England	0.1	*	*	0.1	0.3
Mid-Atlantic	0.3	0.1	0.2	0.3	1.0
Eastern Midwest	*	0.1	0.1	0.1	0.9
Northern Midwest	*	*	*	*	*
Southern Midwest	*	0.7	0.3	0.3	0.5
Upper South Atlantic	2.0	2.2	2.1	1.9	1.7
Southeast	1.8	2.9	3.8	4.2	2.0
Eastern South Central	0.8	2.1	2.7	2.9	1.8
Western South Central	*	2.5	2.5	2.0	1.4
California, Southwest	*	*	*	*	0.6

Source: U.S. Bureau of the Census, *Historical Statistics of the United States* (Washington, D.C., 1961), p. 12.

a. The value of 1.0 indicates that the proportion of an ethnic group living in a given region equaled the proportion of the total national population living in the region. Values below 1.0 indicate underrepresentation and values above 1.0 overrepresentation.

* Values less than 0.1.

and another 5 percent in its southern and northern sections. The population of the South Central regions had increased slightly to about 19 percent, but this proportion declined thereafter. Because foreign immigration expanded only gradually in the 1820s and 1830s, the western populations were drawn predominantly from the eastern states. Almost 80 percent of the American-born population of Wisconsin in 1850 had originated in New England or the Mid-Atlantic region, and almost 90 percent of the American-born in Mississippi had come from the Southeast and Eastern South Central regions. The people of Missouri, on the other hand, had come from more diverse sources: about 48 percent from the Eastern South Central region, nearly 19 percent from the Upper South Atlantic region, and about 15 percent from the Eastern Midwest.

The distinctive regional patterns of denominational affiliations are another indication of the selective latitudinal pattern of westward migration from the Atlantic Coast. The association of denomination and region was and is a marked trait in defining the different ethnic identities of the descendants of colonial migrants who selectively occupied the West and Southwest, although the absence of reliable data confine discussion of the subject to speculative observations. Baptists predominated throughout the newly settled South Central states, whereas Congregationalists, in keeping with the northerly trajectory of the Yankee movement westward, were prominent only in the northern sections of the Midwest. Religious affiliations in the southern sections of the Midwest and northern sections of the South Central region were extremely mixed, but the strong representation of Methodists and Presbyterians indicated the Mid-Atlantic and Upper South Atlantic origins of these populations.

1850–1890

Around the middle of the 19th century, the volume of foreign immigration increased sharply, as substantial numbers of western Europeans responded to famine or deteriorating economic conditions at home by crossing the Atlantic. Although the Catholic Irish and the Germans predominated, Scandinavians, Dutch, Swiss, and French immigrants, as well as British, entered the United States in large numbers. As early as 1850 the patterns of regional distribution established by the earlier immigrants attracted the majority of those who followed. The Irish were strongly overrepresented in New England and the Mid-Atlantic region, the Germans in the Mid-Atlantic and Midwest regions, and the Scandinavians, Dutch, and Swiss immigrants in the Midwest. The English and Scots were well represented in all those regions, but the Welsh, scarcely evident in New England, were more strongly represented than either the English or Scots in the Mid-Atlantic states.

Although very few foreign immigrants settled in the South, New Orleans as a major port attracted groups that added to the distinctive ethnic composition of the Western South Central region, already characterized by the considerable French-speaking population of Acadians (Nova Scotians). Spanish, French, Italian, and Portuguese immigrants were all overrepresented there. Across the continent, San Francisco also attracted substantial numbers of the same groups, thus accounting for the early overrepresentation of Latin Europeans in California and the Southwest. These patterns of overrepresentation were short-lived in the Western South Central region but persisted longer in California. Of this group of Latin-European nationalities, the Portuguese alone were overrepresented elsewhere, specifically in New England.

These distinctive distributional patterns record differences in Old World circumstances, in routes of migration, and in the ability to respond to American opportunities. The commercial links of New Orleans and San Francisco with European ports accounted for their initially diverse populations. For example, the Portuguese settled in California and southern New England because of American trading connections with the Atlantic islands belonging to Portugal. Many Irish immigrants came as ballast on lumber ships returning to New Brunswick and then found their way to New England and New York by coastal packet or on foot. Somewhat less impoverished were those German and Scandinavian immigrants who had farmed small holdings at home but had been faced with stiff competition from larger landholders. They heard about the Midwest from agents of railroad companies offering land grants and from agents of states that needed more population. Thus many of the continental immigrants were attracted directly to the interior. Many Germans who had sailed on tobacco ships returning from Bremen to Baltimore or on cotton ships returning from Le Havre to New Orleans went straight to the Ohio and middle Mississippi valleys, but larger numbers concentrated in the newly settled Northern Midwest. Immigration from Scandinavia peaked somewhat later, when the settlement of the Northern Midwest was proceeding rapidly. The Scandinavian groups moved directly to the interior in even larger proportions than the Germans.

Europe was not the only source of immigration to the United States during this period: Canada, Mexico, and later Asia contributed substantially to the stream. Canadian immigrants were extremely diverse, comprising Newfoundlanders, French Canadians, and Maritimers; many of the last group were descendants of New Englanders who had moved north around the time of the Revolution. In addition, many Irish and British immigrants who had obtained cheap passage to British America moved down to the American republic. New England and, to a lesser degree, New York were the leading recipients of this migration. The Midwest also received Canadian immigrants, some of whom may have been the descendants of Americans who had preferred the northern to the southern shore of Lake Erie in their westward migration.

Mexican settlement in the Western South Central region proved to be more enduring than that of Latin-European immigrants. In this region, as well as in California and the Southwest, some of the Mexican population was obtained by annexation rather than migration. Only modest numbers of Asian immigrants had entered the United States by 1850, and they were concentrated almost exclusively on the Pacific Coast. Their overrepresentation diminished when other groups moved west and when Asian exclusion legislation in the 1880s curtailed their migration. The final stages of relocation of American Indians on western reservations also occurred in the 1880s, and their declining population began to stabilize. During the first six decades of the 19th century, the number of American Indians had dropped from a half to a quarter of a million; the rate of decline slowed thereafter, and the trend was reversed early in the 20th century.

Table 2.6 shows that between 1850 and 1890 the proportions of the population living in the Midwest and the West increased, and the proportion living in the Northeast and the South diminished. The regional destinations of immigrants strongly influenced these changes. In 1890 the blacks were as highly concentrated in the South as they had been in 1850, though they had been legally free to move since the end of the Civil War. As Table 2.7 reveals, their overrepresentation in the Southeast and Eastern South Central regions actually increased as a result of the westward movement of whites and the avoidance of the South by foreign immigrants.

1890–1920

As the first decade of the 20th century approached, the well-established sources of foreign immigration—the British Isles and continental northwestern Europe—continued to supply large numbers of newcomers. Their proportionate contribution, however, was greatly diminished by the rapid growth of immigration from southern and eastern Europe. Most but not all southern and eastern Europeans settled in fewer regions than did the earlier groups, except the Irish. After 1890 the highly industrialized cities of southern New England, the Mid-Atlantic region, and the Eastern Midwest were the chief destinations of the Italians and the various peoples of the Austro-Hungarian and Russian empires. By 1920 the portion of the total U.S. population living in the Mid-Atlantic region, which received most of these immigrants, had slightly increased after a century of decline (see Table 2.6). The census tabulations of the diverse ethnic groups coming from the Russian and Austro-Hungarian empires were rarely consistent, and it is difficult to obtain a precise determination of their regional concentrations. Nevertheless, data for 1890 reveal that, as was the case with the immigrants from northwestern Europe, the pioneering immigrants from southern and eastern Europe had already established enduring regional destinations. By that date the more dispersed patterns of Czech migrants and the secondary concentrations of Italians in New England and of Poles in the Midwest were apparent. In addition, both the South and the more rural sections of the Midwest were losing migrants to the more urbanized parts of the country.

After 1890 the population of the West continued to grow rapidly. While southern Europeans were well represented in California by 1920, most eastern European groups were underrepresented. Asian immigration, restricted in the 1880s, rose again after the turn of the century and remained highly concentrated in California and the Pacific Northwest. The growth of substantial Chinese communities in the cities of the Northeast was already apparent, however, and the Chinese were overrepresented in the Mid-Atlantic region. Mexican immigration, which had never been large in the 19th century, increased sixfold in the decade of World War I, at least in part as a result of the diminished supply of European labor. During this decade also, black Americans moved to the Northeast and Midwest in large numbers. During earlier decades, and especially in the 1890s, small numbers of blacks had moved to northern cities, but these movements were swamped by the immensity of European immigration. By 1920 the Mid-Atlantic region and the Eastern Midwest contained over 10 percent of the black population; however, 85 percent of all blacks continued to live in the four southern regions. The regional patterns of Canadian migration were also maintained; the concentration in New England of more than 70 percent of French Canadians was the highest of any group in any one region.

Differences in dominant regional destinations of foreign immigrants before and after 1890 were among the criteria used by contemporary observers to distinguish the "old" immigration from the "new." Old immigrants were assumed to be from cultures similar to that of the United States, and their presumed rapid assimilation into American society was thought to have been facilitated by their widespread distribution and their settlement on the land as well as in the cities. These assumptions certainly did not apply to the Irish, the second largest immigrant group of the period before 1890, who were as highly concentrated in cities and in the Northeast as any of the new immigrants. Moreover, even though the Germans, the largest group of old immigrants, were more evenly distributed than the Irish between the Atlantic Coast and the Midwest, their group consciousness in the 19th century was as strong as that of any new ethnic group.

A large proportion of the new immigrants from southern and eastern Europe were indeed concentrated in northeastern industrial cities, where native-born Americans were a minority. That these immigrants settled primarily in cities is often attributed to their ignorance of opportunities elsewhere and their lack of occupational skills. In fact, it was the demand for unskilled labor, however poorly paid, that attracted most of them to urban centers. Although the unscrupulous promotional activities of transportation companies were a factor in the increased volume and distant sources of the new immigration, few immigrants were influenced primarily by corporate inducements. Most newcomers joined friends and relatives who were already established in the New World. The observers who made a distinction between new and old immigration did not understand the effects of length of residence in the United States on both the distribution and assimilation of immigrants, nor did they recognize the major differences in the locational characteristics of individual groups.

Table 2.8 shows the high proportions of urban residents among immigrants from southern and eastern Europe in 1920—over 80 percent for most. Among immigrant groups from northwestern Europe, the proportions were less than 75 percent, except for the Irish, who remained one of the most highly urbanized immigrant groups throughout the entire period of mass immigration. Almost 87 percent of the people of Irish birth lived in cities, a proportion exceeded only by people born in the Russian Empire.

Table 2.8. Urban concentration of first-generation white population, by country of origin, 1920 (by percentage).

Country of origin	Urban percentage of whole group	Percentage of total first-generation white urban population
Russian Empire	88.6	12.0
Ireland	86.9	8.7
Italy	84.4	13.1
Poland	84.4	9.3
Hungary	80.0	2.9
United Kingdom	75.0	8.4
Austria	75.0	4.2
Canada	74.5	8.1
Yugoslavia	69.3	1.1
Germany	67.5	12.3
Czechoslovakia	66.3	2.3
Scandinavia	54.6	7.7
Others	—	9.9

Source: Niles Carpenter, *Immigrants and Their Children*, U.S. Bureau of the Census Monograph No. 7 (Washington, D.C., 1927), p. 372, table 167.

The contributions of several other old immigrant groups to the total immigrant population of all cities remained substantial in 1920. For example, only 67.5 percent of German immigrants lived in cities, but because the German group was so large it accounted for more than 12 percent of the total foreign-born white population in American cities. Only Italian immigrants, of whom more than 84 percent were urban residents, outnumbered Germans in the foreign-born urban population. Similarly, people from the United Kingdom, Canada, and Scandinavia together accounted for nearly 25 percent of the total number of urban immigrants. Thus, although many ethnic and national groups of the new immigration settled almost exclusively in cities, only those from Italy and the Russian Empire contributed substantially more people to American cities than did most of the groups of the old immigration.

1920–Present

In the 1920s Congress enacted a series of laws designed to check the flow of immigrants to the United States, laws that openly discriminated against newcomers. The immigration quotas remained in effect, with some slight modifications, until 1965. They compounded the effects of declining population growth and improved living standards in those parts of Europe that had supplied the most immigrants before 1890. Because the countries with generous quotas were no longer major sources of emigration, the total volume of European migration to the United States was greatly reduced.

Despite the proverbial spatial mobility of Americans and the fading out of many overt ethnic traits in the children of immigrants, the regional patterns of most ethnic groups, often established early in the group's immigration, have been remarkably persistent. One striking exception to this stability of ethnic distributions over the past 50 years has been the reduced overrepresentation of northwestern Europeans in the Midwest and their increased representation on the Pacific coast. These groups have contributed greatly to the general migration to the West, especially the Pacific coast.

But by far the most conspicuous distributional change over the past half-century has been the movement of blacks to the Northeast and Midwest. In 1920 85 percent of all blacks were still concentrated in the South, but by 1970 the proportion had been reduced by half. More recently the Southwest and California have become leading destinations of black migrants, and an ebb tide of black movement back to the South may be beginning. Southern whites have also moved to the North and West in large numbers. Southern California has attracted numbers of people from the Eastern and Western South Central states as well as from the Midwest. In the past 15 years, too, the once isolated sections of

Appalachia have become a source of white southern migration to the cities of the Midwest. The rate of Mexican immigration has also increased in the recent past, but the pattern of regional concentration has scarcely changed. Only recently has the immigration of Puerto Ricans and Cubans been substantial, with the resulting concentration of the former group in New York and the latter in Florida.

Thus the current regional ethnic group patterns are the result of an incremental process in which both the composition and destinations of migrants have changed. Each major immigrant group established an initial pattern of concentration, and subsequent migrants tended to choose the same destinations, attracted by networks of information and the sense of security generated by the presence of their compatriots. Often the initial clusters represented new employment opportunities that happened to coincide with the arrival of a particular group, or, alternatively, the skills and enterprise of a newly arrived group were particularly appropriate to a growing sector of the economy. Not all immigrant groups, however, had the appropriate skills or arrived at the right time. Emigrants who left their homeland because of famine, acute agricultural distress, or repression probably had little control over their destination. Nevertheless, a rudimentary ethnic division of labor emerged, in which certain groups dominated certain kinds of employment and tended to cluster in certain regions or cities. Long after this ethnic division of labor had begun to lose its rigidity, group concentrations were maintained by institutional and family ties. In short, both social and economic factors encouraged the concentrations of ethnic groups in the United States, and the well-defined if overlapping regional clusters of most of these groups have persisted to this day.

Changing Urban Patterns

The large-scale regional distributions of American ethnic groups have been far more persistent than their urban residential patterns. By the late 19th century, the city had become the leading destination of all migrants, and the descendants of many people who had settled on the land in the middle decades of the century joined the cityward movement. The first observers of the urban experiences of migrants spoke of a kind of "elevator" of material advancement and assimilation, from initial residence in ethnically well-defined inner-city slums to suburbs with no obvious ethnic identification. This view acknowledged that the rate of advancement varied from group to group and that not all groups entered on the ground floor. Today we are aware, however, that the elevator generalization may not have applied to some groups, and further, that assimilation and suburbanization do not have a simple relationship. The elevator image was formulated during the early decades of the present century when large numbers of new immigrants were congregating in the inner cities and when some old immigrants and their descendants were moving to the suburbs. Although residence in an inner-city slum seemed to be a temporary part of the immigrant's experience in America, it was viewed as a symbol of the failure of the American dream, not only in regard to material conditions and opportunities but also because it spawned political corruption and threatened democracy.

More recent interpretations view the immigrants' urban experiences and their inner-city neighborhoods in a more positive light, emphasizing the value of ethnic institutions and family networks in helping immigrants adapt to their new country. Even 19th-century political corruption is seen as an informal and undemeaning welfare arrangement at a time when bureaucratic social services were undeveloped. The newer interpretations also reveal that there was a great range of inner-city social and material conditions and that although each ethnic quarter housed most of a group's institutions, it was not necessarily the dominant point of concentration for the group. In addition, the inner city, despite its congested housing, offered locational advantages to immigrants who were employed in an adjacent central business district. Because immigrant employment was often uncertain and seasonal or entailed awkward hours, even cheap local transportation was no substitute for the opportunity to walk or cycle to work. These reevaluations of the role of inner-city ethnic quarters, however, are appropriate only to the experiences of groups who moved to American cities in the late 19th and early 20th centuries. They are not generally applicable to (1) the masses of immigrants who arrived before the Civil War, (2) the South, or (3) those groups, mainly blacks, who dominate inner cities today.

In the first case, the conditions leading to urban segregation were lacking before the Civil War. The concentration of immigrants in central sections depended upon the abandonment of housing, or at least of space, by previous residents and upon locally available employment. Only during the 1870s and 1880s did the suburban movement reach such a scale that it released an adequate supply of centrally located housing to meet the needs of immigrant newcomers. Immigrants could be housed at increased densities, but before the 1870s they quickly filled the available central space, and many were forced to live on the edge of the city and on undesirable sites avoided by more prosperous residents. During the 1850s especially, when most eastern cities could not house the large numbers of newly arrived immigrants, many German and Irish newcomers were obliged to set up peripheral shantytowns similar to those common today in less-developed areas of the world. It was in the newer cities of the interior—where the number of immigrants often approached, equaled, or exceeded that of the native-born—that, in the absence of preexisting housing, large, contiguous inner-city concentrations could be established. In mid-19th-century cities, too, employment was characteristically scattered and small in scale, and the still-developing manufacturing and commercial districts were not always the most important sources of jobs. Only toward the close of the century were the majority of immigrant groups and the leading sources of their employment concentrated in central urban locations.

Second, both before and after the Civil War cities in the

South exhibited distinctive residential patterns, partly because the South attracted proportionately few foreign immigrants and partly because blacks were a major element in their populations. Extensive areas of segregation were rare; blacks often lived in the back alleys and rear lots of neighborhoods whose main streets were inhabited by whites. Thus clusters of blacks were dotted throughout southern cities, not concentrated in one well-defined black quarter. Even in border and northern cities, black populations often were widely scattered.

Third, when the blacks flooded northern cities during World War I, extensive and contiguous black quarters developed. Since most inner-city residential quarters in the North were already densely occupied by European immigrants, the expansion of black areas was limited to districts somewhat removed from the city center, where speculative overbuilding for middle-income people had created a supply of cheap dwellings suitable for subdivision. Boston's Roxbury, New York's Harlem, and Chicago's South Side are examples of urban areas that, though not the most centrally located, offered cheap housing to blacks. Subsequently, as other ethnic groups moved to the suburbs and as the black populations continued to grow, the initial black quarters expanded toward the inner city as well as outward. Yet even while larger sections of the inner city were becoming available to blacks, urban employment was becoming decentralized. Consequently, the black residential districts have remained well removed from the centers of employment.

The deprivation of blacks and other newcomers to American cities in recent decades is a result not only of their high levels of residential segregation but also of the timing of their arrival in relation to the changing locations of urban employment and changing employment opportunities. The persistence of distinctive regional and urban spatial patterns among groups is a record of the enduring effects of ethnicity in residential locations, but relative location in the city or region provides only a partial key to the material and social situation of each ethnic group.

3

A HISTORY OF U.S. IMMIGRATION POLICY

In the nearly four centuries since the English first settled in Jamestown, over 45 million people have immigrated to the United States or to the colonies out of which the nation grew, and from the earliest years immigration has been of concern to the makers of public policy. Americans have sought to stimulate and regulate the flow of newcomers in a variety of ways. U.S. immigration policy has been a sensitive barometer both of the achievements and of the problems of national development, for it has been quick to respond to changing economic, political, social, and diplomatic circumstances. The history of American immigration policy falls into five distinct periods: the colonial era (1609–1775); the Open Door era (1776–1881); the era of regulation (1882–1916); the era of restriction (1917–1964); and the era of liberalization (1965 to the present).

The Colonial Period, 1609–1775

In the 17th century the English drive for overseas empire shaped the patterns of immigration and settlement in the North American colonies. The process of peopling the

American continent was deliberate and organized, for population was needed to cultivate the virgin lands of the New World—population that would enable colonies to supply raw materials to the mother country and would consume its manufactured goods.

From the early 17th century to the American Revolution, colonial immigration policy was carried out on two levels: on one, the government of the empire—the Crown, Parliament, the Board of Trade—regulated the activities of the North American colonies; on the other, the colonial governments—legislatures, proprietors, and local officials—enacted and enforced laws within the imperial framework. On occasion the two levels came into conflict. In the 1660s, for example, when Parliament approved the transportation of convicted felons to the Chesapeake Bay area—considering that putting them to work in the labor-short colonies was more productive than executing or imprisoning them—the Virginia assembly, fearful of social disturbances, decreed that "no person trading with Virginia, either by land or sea, should bring in any 'jailbirds.'" Maryland in 1676 enacted a similar exclusionary law, but Parliament overruled the restrictions, and private contractors continued to arrange the transportation of convicts to those colonies into the 18th century.

On the whole, however, the consensus at both levels of government was that the goal of immigration policy was the recruitment of labor. It was left to colonial governments and entrepreneurs to devise schemes to attract people to the colonies and thereby increase property values, rents, and profits. To do this they advertised the opportunities of the New World to the people of the British Isles and Europe in a variety of ways. In 1609 the Virginia Company launched a publicity drive in London; its advertisements, preached from the pulpits, generated a flurry of gentry investment and volunteering for colonization. In the late 17th century, Anthony Ashley Cooper, the proprietor of the Carolinas, publicized throughout the West Indies and Europe the abundant land

and the religious toleration that could be found there. William Penn made Pennsylvania the most widely advertised of all the colonies: he himself went to Europe to supervise recruitment campaigns and distributed hundreds of pamphlets and advertisements in English, French, German, and Dutch announcing that Pennsylvania had given all males the right to vote, had enacted a humane penal code, and required no military service.

Colonial governments provided not only information about, but transportation to, the colonies and subsidized purchase of lands and tools for new settlers as well. The Puritans of Massachusetts Bay helped pay for the transportation, food, and equipment of recruits to their Holy Commonwealth. The Calverts of Maryland, Cooper of the Carolinas, and Penn dipped into family fortunes to stock the colonists with equipment and supplies, and sold land to new arrivals at low prices. By extending this helpful hand to enterprising immigrants, they provided them from the very beginning with a substantial stake in the settlement.

Colonies also offered "bounties" to recruiting agents who provided settlers. As early as 1678 South Carolina was paying bounties to importers of white servants, sometimes to the master of a vessel who brought the newcomers, and sometimes to immigration agents called "importers." These schemes for recruitment and transportation stimulated the first great wave of colonization in the Chesapeake Bay area. The Virginia Company pioneered the practice of indentured servitude, and in the 17th century brought an average of 1,500 bonded laborers each year to the Chesapeake Bay. An indentured servant bound himself to the company or to a planter for four to seven years; in return he received free passage, a year's provisions, a house and tools, and a share of the crops he produced. When his contract expired, he gained all the rights of a freeman and the opportunity to hold title to his own land. In 1619 the company established the "headright" system to promote still more immigration. The headright conferred upon a person a title to 50 acres of uncultivated land upon arrival in Virginia or, if he was already there, for paying the transportation costs of another settler who would discharge the obligation by working on his land. Dedicated to reforming the English church and to building a regenerate society, the Puritans of the New England colonies limited their recruitment to fellow religious communicants of the gentry, yeoman, tradesman, and artisan classes of England. They sought family men with useful skills who could help build the community; they excluded or expelled itinerants, adventurers, Quakers, and members of other religious sects of which they did not approve. They spurned the mass advertising employed by the proprietary colonies and Virginia, relying for selection instead on the quiet working of religious inspiration. Since the Puritan polity tied civil government to ecclesiastical goals, full political and civil rights were granted only to the members of their church. The Puritan New England colonies were the most socially homogeneous settlements in America; religious orthodoxy functioned both as a process of selection and as a restriction on the numbers who came.

By 1700 nearly all the colonies were employing some combination of advertising, grants of land, employment incentives, transportation payment, and guarantee of rights and freedoms to increase the flow of immigrants; informal naturalization laws permitted aliens to secure freehold land (land without restrictions on transfer) once they had arrived. Like a giant magnet, the colonies drew farmers, workers, artisans, and tradesmen who had been dislodged by a changing European economy. Although the availability of work was the primary inducement, the religious policy of most of the colonies was an additional attraction. Outside New England's restrictive establishment, toleration of all Christian denominations, and even of Judaism, was gradually established. Some proprietors marked their colonies as havens for particular groups seeking protection from religious persecution: Lord Calvert made Maryland an asylum for England's Catholics; William Penn turned Pennsylvania into a sanctuary for Quakers and others; the strict orthodoxy of New England made its settlements the destination of those seeking an uncompromisingly reformed English church—though even in New England a degree of tolerance had been accorded to non-Congregationalists by 1700. Religious conformity itself declined throughout the 18th century. Without coercive authority, secure leadership, and state sanctions, religion became a matter of choice with little formal relevance to civil status, and religious tests for entry into any of the colonies soon fell into disuse.

The attraction of the New World for non-British groups was increased after 1740 by a major shift in policy toward arriving aliens. Until that year, colonial governments granted deeds of "denization," or naturalization, to aliens that bestowed civil and property-holding rights preliminary to full British citizenship. To speed up settlement, letters of naturalization were even issued to aliens in England. These deeds, however, were not binding upon the imperial government and were often not honored by the colonies. In 1740 Parliament cleared the ambiguous status of aliens by passing a universal naturalization act that made all aliens in the colonies fully naturalized British subjects as soon as they could prove that they had resided continuously on British territory for seven years.

Changes in the land-distribution policy of the colonies in the 18th century further stimulated the flow of newcomers. The headright system had concentrated an excessive amount of land in the hands of a few prosperous merchants and speculators, so in 1705 the Virginia legislature dismantled the program and introduced a system of direct government sale of land warrants to settlers at low prices; Maryland and the Carolinas soon followed the same course. In New England the practice of deeding land only to acceptable religious groups collapsed under the pressure of popular demand for new uncultivated areas. Land speculators obtained whole townships from the General Court of Massachusetts in the 1720s and, in the 1740s, held public auctions of New

England land. The proprietors of the huge virgin-land tracts in the Northern Neck of Virginia, the hinterland of Pennsylvania, the Carolinas, and Maryland distributed freehold land at public sales and opened settlement unconditionally to all comers.

Three features of immigration policy that would shape 19th-century patterns were established in the colonial period. First, it was local government that exercised jurisdiction over immigration and settlement. Second, the central government left it to local governments and entrepreneurs to recruit immigrants from other countries. Finally, the increasing demands of economic development led to a search for new sources of labor—a search that would spread in the 19th century into countries unimagined by Tudor Englishmen or colonial planters.

The Open Door Era, 1776–1881

The rejection by the British government of colonial demands for a more open immigration policy to attract newcomers was one of the many grievances that led colonists to take up arms against the British in 1775. The Declaration of Independence attacked the king and the Privy Council for endeavoring "to prevent the population of these states" by refusing to recognize general naturalization acts passed by colonial assemblies and by restricting westward settlement in the Proclamation of 1763 and the Quebec Act of 1774. As the Revolution progressed it also brought with it a new concept of national identity. In their struggle to separate themselves from Englishmen, Americans began to see themselves as a unique people bred from the frontier and from the mingling of several nationalities. The popular writer Tom Paine wrote in 1776, "Europe, and not England, is the parent country of America." By then more than a third of the country's white inhabitants were of nonEnglish origin.

The Philadelphia convention that drafted the Constitution of the United States in 1787 debated the question of immigration. Alexander Hamilton, a West Indian by birth, argued that immigrants could make important contributions to the welfare of the nation and that they should be regarded as "on the level of the first citizens." George Mason of Virginia agreed, saying he "was for opening a wide door for emigrants," but hesitated "to let foreigners . . . make laws for us and govern us." Pierce Butler of South Carolina and Gouverneur Morris of Pennsylvania feared that immigrants would retain the political principles of the despotic countries they had left behind. Despite these reservations, however, the framers of the Constitution ended by making the foreign-born ineligible only for the presidency; senators had to be citizens for nine years or more, and representatives for seven. Congress was also empowered to establish a uniform naturalization law.

Many leaders of the new republic clearly expected the immigrant to play a major role in the development of the nation. In the Northwest Ordinance of 1787, Congress guaranteed religious freedom in the Northwest Territories, hoping that this liberty would be an added attraction for immigrants. "That part of America which has encouraged [the foreigners] most, has advanced most rapidly in population, agriculture and the arts," observed James Madison, while Hamilton declared that "a perfect equality of religious privileges will probably cause [immigrants] to flock from Europe to the United States," and Assistant Secretary of State Tench Coxe composed notes for the information of the immigrant which endorsed the freedom of religion in the United States and promised that freedom to all.

The American Revolution and the Napoleonic wars hindered the flow of immigration until 1815. In the intervening period Congress passed (1790) the first federal laws loosely defining a uniform rule for the naturalization of aliens: any free white person who resided for two years "within the limits and under the jurisdiction of the United States" could acquire American citizenship. The review of naturalization applications was to be made by "any common law court of record in any one of the States." These generous terms for citizenship and open immigration laid the basis for the massive growth of population that was to follow in the next century.

But the political struggles of the new nation also led to the first, though ultimately unsuccessful, effort to impede the assimilation of newcomers. In 1798 the Federalist party secured the passage of the Alien Act designed to harass immigrants who they suspected might become Republicans, and to deny them the vote by raising the residency requirement for citizenship to 14 years. Three years later, after the Republican victory in the election of 1800, the act was repealed in favor of a 5-year residency requirement.

Authority over immigration continued to be exercised mainly by state governments and local officials until after the Civil War. In practice the regulation of immigrant traffic was assumed by those states having large ports, such as Massachusetts, New York, Pennsylvania, and Maryland. From 1820 to 1860 these states passed laws to reduce the social and financial costs of monitoring immigration. New York, where two-thirds of all newcomers landed, pioneered inspection and welfare laws and required shipmasters to report the name, occupation, birthplace, age, and physical condition of each passenger. On the basis of these reports, the infirm and the destitute who might become wards of the state could be identified and deported. Bond had to be posted for any immigrant suspected of being a potential charity case. New York also charged each shipmaster $1.50 for cabin passengers and $1.00 for those in steerage; the fees paid were used to maintain a marine hospital. Massachusetts ordered shipmasters transporting immigrants to pay $2.00 for each passenger to the city of Boston; those fees were used for support of those foreigners who, after admission, became paupers. To execute these laws the coastal states established immigration boards; run by social reformers and humanitarians who served without pay, their enforcement procedures tended to be casual.

New York's state laws requiring the screening of immigrants were challenged in a landmark U.S. Supreme Court case, *City of New York v. Milne* (1837), in which the defendant Milne, the master of a ship that transported immigrants, argued that the New York regulations were an obstruction of interstate and foreign commerce. The Supreme Court, however, found that the laws derived from the legitimate right of states to exercise police power within their boundaries: "We think it as competent for a State to provide precautionary measures against the moral pestilence of paupers, vagabonds, and possibly convicts, as it is to guard against the physical pestilence which may arise from unsound or infectious articles imported, or from a ship, the crew of which may be laboring under an infectious disease," the opinion read. This decision authorized state governments to set criteria for the suitability of immigrants for admission and to reject arrivals who did not meet their standards.

The processing of new arrivals in the mid-19th century was best exemplified by the procedures used at Castle Garden, the immigration depot of New York City between 1855 and 1890. Converted from a former opera house at the southern tip of Manhattan, Castle Garden provided reception and orientation services, a hospital where sick passengers could recuperate before venturing forth, an inexpensive restaurant, free baths, baggage-carrying services, and a communal kitchen. The commissioners of Castle Garden served without pay, compiling employment listings, arranging for transportation, and even licensing numerous boarding houses to which they could direct immigrants who needed lodging. They gave a brief medical examination to all passengers, recorded names, ages, occupations, religions, and the value of the belongings they brought into the country. Castle Garden was run as if it were a protective charity foundation: it provided safety from swindlers and confidence men, a hospitable reception for the newcomers, practical advice, and social services. The spirit of benevolence guided the welfare workers on its all-volunteer staff.

During the first half of the 19th century the federal government did little to supervise, control, or promote immigration. Federal officials kept no records of immigrants until 1820, when the State Department first began to count the number of immigrant entrants each year. The tasks of recruiting immigrants and adjusting the newcomers to American life when they arrived were assumed by local governments and by entrepreneurs; the federal government simply relied on the open land market and other advantages and opportunities to attract immigrants.

The expanding frontier and industrializing cities continued to demand manpower. Several western states sent brochures and pamphlets overseas describing the opportunities to purchase public land at $1.25 an acre. In 1845 Michigan appointed an agent to recruit immigrants on the docks of New York City. Wisconsin followed suit, and also organized county committees to compile mailing lists of the settlers' friends and relatives still in Europe. Minnesota hired a clerk to draw up mailing lists and to send advertisements to Europe in English, Welsh, German, Dutch, Norwegian, and Swedish; it had a publicity agent covering Sweden and another stationed in Bremen, who visited shipping offices and emigrant boarding houses; and it awarded prizes for the essays that were judged best at describing opportunities in the state for the immigrant. These essays were published in seven languages and distributed in the appropriate countries of Europe.

In the second half of the 19th century, 33 state and territorial governments established immigration offices to attract newcomers. Their pamphlets extolled the virtues of the American frontier and of its allegedly salubrious climate. An Iowa pamphlet of 1870 described the beauty of an Iowan Indian summer; Minnesota pointed out that its death rate was only a fourth or a third of that in Europe. The theme most emphasized, however, was the contrast between American opportunity and European stagnation. The Iowa pamphlet declared that in the Midwest men could become prosperous and independent, while in Europe "the great majority . . . must live out their days as dependent labourers on the land of others." Minnesota's pamphlet proclaimed, "It is well to exchange the tyrannies and thankless toil of the old world for the freedom and independence of the new . . . it is well for the hand of labour to bring forth the rich treasures hid in the bosom of the NEW EARTH." The competition for immigrants also inspired a fierce rivalry between states. Wisconsin charged that Minnesota was farther away, had fewer railroads, and more frequent natural disasters. Iowa and Minnesota disparaged the Dakotas, with their locusts, Indians, blizzards, and droughts.

As the flow of arriving immigrants increased, policy makers slowly began to realize that the federal government was going to have to devote greater attention to the new arrivals; in 1855 Congress directed officials of the U.S. Customs Service to compile both quarterly and annual immigration reports. In 1864 Congress passed a bill establishing a Bureau of Immigration, but in 1867 it transferred the job of keeping immigration records to the more technically capable Bureau of Statistics in the Treasury Department.

The first federal attempt at direct promotion of immigration was made in 1864, with a contract-labor law that authorized employers to finance the transportation of immigrant workers and to bind their services in advance, but the measure was repealed in 1868 in the face of protests from labor organizations.

The Republican party became the major advocate for a stronger federal immigration policy. The Republican platform of 1864 asserted: "Foreign immigration which in the past has added so much to the wealth, resources, and increase of power to this nation—the asylum of the oppressed of all nations—should be fostered and encouraged by a liberal and just policy"; in 1868 and 1872 the Republican party reaffirmed this plank.

A dispute in 1874 over the coming of Mennonite (Amish) immigrants nearly pushed Congress into an unprecedented policy, as congressmen debated a proposal to reserve a huge tract of western land for thousands of Mennonites as an inducement for them to come to the United States rather than to Canada. Opponents of the plan argued successfully that no group should receive preferential treatment on the basis of "a special right to compact themselves as an exclusive community." The controversy ended when three western states offered the Mennonites exemption from military duty and thereby lured most of them to the United States.

By the 1870s over 280,000 immigrants a year were disembarking at American ports. The highest levels of government could no longer afford to be diffident or to entrust to the states the management of the powerful force of immigration. In 1875, a United States Supreme Court decision inaugurated a major revision in national immigration policy. In *Henderson* v. *Mayor of New York,* a case raising issues identical to those in *New York* v. *Milne,* the Supreme Court reversed its 1837 decision: the justices now declared that all existing state laws regulating immigration were unconstitutional on the grounds that they usurped the exclusive power vested in Congress to regulate foreign commerce. The justices concluded by calling for federal supervision of immigration:

> It is equally clear that the matter of these statutes may be, and ought to be, the subject of a uniform system or plan. The laws which govern the right to land passengers in the United States from other countries ought to be the same in New York, Boston, New Orleans, and San Francisco . . . We are of the opinion that this whole subject has been confided to Congress by the Constitution; that Congress can more appropriately and with more acceptance exercise it than any other body known to our law, state or national; that by providing a system of laws in these matters, applicable to all ports and to all vessels, a serious question, which has long been a matter of contest and complaint, may be effectually and satisfactorily settled.

This decision at first threw the burden of receiving foreigners and discouraging unfit immigrants onto private philanthropic organizations, because a federal agency to perform these functions had not yet been established. Overwhelmed by the growing volume of immigrants and the strain on their resources, charity workers soon petitioned Congress to authorize federal action. In the 1880s Congress enacted a series of statutes bringing immigration under direct federal control and—a measure that proved to be more significant—allowing the federal government to exercise its authority to restrict the entry of people thought to be undesirable.

The Era of Regulation, 1882–1916

In the late 19th century the federal government built the administrative and bureaucratic machinery that would operate this new federal immigration policy. Policy makers began to experiment with new ways of monitoring arrivals, so that only those thought to be most adaptable to American society would be admitted. As concern about social problems thought to be the result of immigration mounted, they gradually constructed regulations that admitted only those who were healthy and employable.

The drive for federal regulation of immigration originated in California, where Chinese immigrants had begun to arrive around the time of the gold rush of 1849; many more came to the West Coast in the ensuing years, largely as contract labor brought in to build the railroads. By 1869, 63,000 Chinese had come to the United States, and twice that number arrived in the course of the next decade. Public reaction to the mounting numbers led the government of California to experiment with laws that would cut down the rate of entry. As early as 1852 the governor and the state assembly were recommending restrictive measures; state courts declared the Chinese ineligible for naturalization on the grounds that they could not be categorized among the "free whites" stipulated by federal law. In 1855 California passed a law levying a $50 capitation tax on arriving passengers ineligible for citizenship. Two years later, however, the U.S. Supreme Court declared this act unconstitutional. In 1870 restrictionists, claiming that Asian prostitutes were being imported into the country, obtained a state law prohibiting the landing of any Mongolian, Japanese, or Chinese female who could not provide evidence of voluntary emigration and decent character. To curb the influx of contract labor, the law was subsequently extended to males.

Nearly all the Chinese who came were unskilled laborers who were willing to work for little pay and who therefore were thought to threaten the wages and working conditions of the locals. Labor organizations, led by the Mechanics State Council of California, decided that state regulation was not sufficient and appealed to the U.S. Congress to place national limits on the immigration of Chinese workers. Republicans and Democrats alike in the far-western states agreed that federal action was required, but this placed the administration in an awkward position: Chinese immigration rights had been formally guaranteed by the Burlingame Treaty between the United States and China (1868), by which, in exchange for certain trade concessions, the U.S. government pledged that it would not restrict the numbers of Chinese workers coming into the country. But in 1879 Congress gave way to pressure from the western states, and in direct violation of that agreement enacted legislation banning from American ports any vessel carrying more than 15 Chinese passengers. President Rutherford B. Hayes vetoed the measure as a violation of international agreement. But the next year a new treaty was negotiated with China which permitted the United States to "regulate, limit, or suspend," but "not absolutely prohibit," the immigration of Chinese laborers, and in 1882 Congress took advantage of the provision to suspend the entry of Chinese workers for ten years. The Chinese Exclusion Act of 1882 stated that restrictions were needed because "in the opinion of the Government of the United States the coming of Chinese laborers to this country endangers the good order of certain localities."

The most radical provision of the law was the one that barred all foreign-born Chinese from acquiring citizenship. The basis for this statute was the Naturalization Act of 1790 in which acquisition of citizenship by naturalization had been limited to "free white persons"; an act of 1870 had subsequently extended the privilege to "aliens of African nativity and persons of African descent." Now, for the first time, a federal statute was designating a group as specifically ineligible on the grounds of race. Chinese immigration had aroused a national effort to identify an unassimilable alien race and to ban it from entry. Although in the 1880s the Chinese issue was kept distinct from the problems arising from European immigration, it nonetheless firmly established the prerogative of the federal government to raise restrictive barriers against specific national groups.

In 1882 Congress enacted the first comprehensive federal immigration law and delegated authority to the Treasury Department for enforcing it, but the states were still left with primary responsibility for the inspection of immigrants to see that all those excluded by law—convicts, lunatics, idiots, and incapacitated persons who might become public charges—were turned back. Carrying on another earlier state practice, immigrant welfare was paid for out of a federal fund raised by levying a charge of 50 cents on each entering alien.

In 1885 Congress passed the Foran Act, another exclusionary law, this time lobbied through Congress by the Knights of Labor. It prohibited the recruitment of unskilled labor by prepaid passage and advance contracting, but it did not affect skilled workers, artisans, or teachers. It was followed in 1888 by a supplemental law that ordered the deportation of alien contract laborers within one year of entry; by this measure the federal government was empowered to specify regulations that could lead to deportation.

At the same time as the groundwork was being laid for the

imposition of federal controls, the character of immigration also began to change, shifting in ways that aroused concern in some quarters and that led to demands for the government to find new solutions. Although immigrants from northern and western Europe remained in the vast majority in the 1880s, newcomers from southern and eastern Europe were becoming increasingly numerous. They were referred to as "new immigrants," a label that soon acquired invidious connotations.

By the 1890s the new immigrants were in the majority—and in most years it was a large majority. Many natives saw them as having peculiar habits and alien cultures. Some began to believe that the Slavs, Jews, Magyars, Sicilians, and others included in the group were innately inferior and racially unassimilable. Popular journals were filled with hostile references to the newcomers. A large foreign-born population only gradually being acculturated was filling the major urban centers. The demands for a more systematic public policy increased. State authorities were calling for federal assistance to process the multitude of immigrants and to facilitate their adjustment. They demanded that minimal health and competency standards be set for the welfare of native and immigrant communities alike. The Progressive movement, bent on the reform of government and industry and the improvement of social services, popularized the notion that government regulation of immigration would make its management more efficient.

In 1891 Congress finally established a permanent administration for the national control of immigration in the form of a superintendent of immigration within the Treasury Department. Minimum health qualifications for immigrants were formulated, as was an effective method for deporting immigrants rejected by U.S. inspectors: steamship companies were now compelled by law to return all unacceptable passengers to their country of origin. Aliens who landed illegally or became public charges within one year of arrival were subject to deportation. The law of 1891 also added new categories to those to be excluded: polygamists were banned, along with "persons suffering from a loathsome or dangerous contagious disease." The exclusion of contract labor was extended by prohibiting employers from advertising abroad for laborers and by preventing laborers responding to illegal advertisements from entering the country. The law of 1891 ushered in full-scale federal control of immigration. Although the regulatory mechanisms operated only on overseas immigrants and did not affect people crossing U.S. borders by land, the state governments were at least no longer responsible for monitoring the stream of foreigners arriving from abroad. Overtaxed charity organizations were relieved of their burden as federal agents began to provide reception services to newcomers.

About three-quarters of the newcomers entered at the port of New York City. The old welcoming station, Castle Garden, was no longer sufficient, so a new federal facility, Ellis Island, was built to take its place. Constructed on the site of an old naval arsenal in 1892, Ellis Island was the gateway to America for millions of immigrants until 1932, when it was turned into a detention center; it was closed in 1954, but refurbished and reopened in 1965 as an immigration museum administered as part of the Statue of Liberty National Monument.

In contrast to the casual paternalism of Castle Garden, Ellis Island was efficient and impersonal. After quarantine and customs procedures immigrants were hustled past doctors, and a matron who examined pregnant women, on an assembly-line basis, each doctor assigned to looking for one specific disease; three special inspectors decided on the doubtful cases. As health regulations were added to the exclusion clauses, the examinations grew more complex and time-consuming. Those who passed were then interviewed by registry clerks who recorded vital statistics and other background information. Finally, the immigrants were sent to special offices housed in the federal station for currency exchange, rail tickets, baggage handling, and telegrams.

If Ellis Island was a symbol of hope and opportunity to millions of newcomers, it was also the symbol of rejection for many others. In the late 1890s, the more stringent examination system annually debarred over 3,000 applicants for admission; by 1910 the number exceeded 24,000. About 15 percent of those sent back were rejected as having contagious diseases, another 15 percent as constituting contract labor, and the remainder as potential charity cases. An organized movement to establish stricter controls over the massive influx of foreigners began to form at about the same time that Ellis Island opened. From 1891 to 1929 Congress erected a complex body of law designed to narrow the range of immigrants who qualified for admission. The course of this evolution of policy was, however, far from smooth. Well into the 20th century, generally speaking, the Democratic party was indifferent or strongly opposed to restriction. The urban electorate of the Northeast and Midwest pressured congressmen to keep immigration as open as possible. Steamship companies and industrialists lobbied for a liberal policy that would assure large cargoes of passengers and a steady supply of cheap labor. Several presidents, from Rutherford B. Hayes to Woodrow Wilson, vetoed congressional bills that would have tightened admissions standards or excluded whole national groups. The evolving immigration policies were the product neither of a coherent plan nor of a systematic philosophy. The total effect, however, was that step by step, requirements for entry were made more and more stringent.

By the turn of the century Congress had already begun to strengthen the administrative apparatus for controlling immigration. In 1893 boards of special inquiry were formed to handle immigration problems and to collect "a list or manifest of alien passengers" entering the United States. In 1906 authority over immigration was transferred from the overburdened Treasury Department to the newly created Department of Commerce and Labor, and a separate Bureau of Immigration and Naturalization was established within that department.

Further refinements and additions were made to the list of excluded. In part a reaction to the assassination of President William McKinley by an anarchist in 1901, but even more a reflection of a widespread fear of "radicals," Congress in 1903 barred anarchists and saboteurs from entry, along with epileptics and professional beggars. Repeated attempts were made to introduce literacy as a requirement for entry, although it would be a long time before these met with any success. The Immigration Restriction League, founded in 1894 by a small group of young Harvard-educated Boston Brahmins, made the literacy requirement its goal for twenty years. In 1896 Massachusetts Senator Henry Cabot Lodge sponsored a bill in Congress that would have excluded any immigrant unable to read 40 words in some language. It was passed by Congress but vetoed by President Grover Cleveland on the grounds that it violated the traditional American policy of free immigration. Other attempts were made in 1898, 1902, and 1906, when the bills did not get through Congress, and in 1913 and 1915, when they did not receive a presidential signature.

The most thoroughgoing restrictions remained those placed on Asian immigration. In 1902 congressmen from the far-western states finally succeeded in having the Chinese Exclusion Act renewed indefinitely, but almost simultaneously the Japanese began arriving in California in numbers as great as those of the Chinese immigrants in their peak years. In reaction, leading businessmen and civic leaders organized the Japanese and Korean Exclusion League in San Francisco (1905), and the movement quickly spread. But again considerations of international diplomacy intervened; the result was the 1907–1908 Gentlemen's Agreement between Japan and the United States that called for voluntary regulation by the Japanese in exchange for the ending of the segregation of Japanese pupils in San Francisco's schools.

At the same time, elsewhere in the country restrictionists were becoming equally disturbed by the numbers of immigrants coming from southern and eastern Europe. In 1910 a congressionally appointed commission headed by a moderate restrictionist, Senator William P. Dillingham of Vermont, issued a 42-volume report on the alarming effects of immigration. It began with the assumption that the new immigrants were racially inferior to the old immigrants from northern and western Europe and manipulated mountains of statistics to provide a "scientific" rationale for restricting their entry. The evidence in fact contradicted the conclusions, but the Dillingham report nonetheless convinced many that southern and eastern Europeans were incapable of becoming Americans and that the best mechanism for restricting their numbers would be the imposition of a literacy test.

The Era of Restriction, 1917–1964

The Immigration Act of 1917 was the first in a series of severely restrictive statutes based on the findings of the Dillingham Commission. A literacy test was finally enacted; all newcomers over 16 years of age who could not pass it were turned back. No laborers were allowed from the so-called Asiatic Barred Zone, which included India, Indochina, Afghanistan, Arabia, the East Indies, and other, smaller Asian countries, but not China and Japan, which were covered by other legal provisions. The act was the first step in establishing a federal policy of restriction wholly based on a rank order of eligible immigrants that favored national groups thought to be most assimilable. Congress overrode the veto of President Wilson, who denounced the act as a violation of American ideals and the traditional Open Door policy.

The literacy test, it soon became clear, would not have its desired effect. In 1921 over 800,000 arrivals were recorded— a total only slightly below the prewar average—and the proportion of southern and eastern Europeans among them remained high. Congress then proceeded to the next step. By the Quota Act of 1921 (the Johnson Act) it limited the annual number of entrants of each admissible nationality to 3 percent of the foreign-born of that nationality as recorded in the U.S. Census of 1910. Quotas were established for countries in Europe, the Near East, and Africa, and for Australia and New Zealand. No limits were placed on immigration from nations in the Western Hemisphere. Congress continued to allow free immigration from its neighbors, partly to maintain good relations, partly yielding to pressure from southwestern agricultural lobbies interested in maintaining the flow of cheap farm labor from Mexico. Southern and eastern European immigration, however, was sharply curtailed; the annual quotas for southern and eastern European countries were in every case less than a quarter of the numbers admitted before World War I.

The principle of special preferences introduced in 1921 was greatly expanded in succeeding years. Preferences—but only within quota limits—were given to "the wives, parents, brothers, sisters, or children under eighteen years of age, and fiancées . . . of citizens of the United States, . . . of aliens now in the United States who have applied for citizenship in the manner provided by law, or . . . of persons eligible for United States citizenship who served in the military or naval forces of the United States [during World War I]." Establishing priorities in the interests of maintaining family unity represented yet another new principle of immigration policy.

The 1921 act also introduced a new class, later referred to as the "nonquota" category, which included aliens returning from visits abroad, professional actors, artists, lecturers, singers, nurses, ministers, and professors. After 1924 all wives and dependent children of U.S. citizens were allowed to enter as nonquota immigrants, as were aliens belonging to any recognized learned profession or employed as domestic servants. All these would be admissible over and above the quotas for the national groups to which they belonged. The nonquota list was extended by subsequent legislation, but the essential point of the original act was its principle that admission could be based on individual characteristics rather that on national quotas. It was to that extent, at least, a liberalizing provision in a law otherwise known only for its restrictionist features.

The law of 1921 was still not rigorous enough for many restrictionists, who, led by Senator Albert Johnson of the state of Washington, soon secured a more draconian measure. The Immigration Act of 1924 (Johnson-Reid Act) reduced the admissible annual total to 165,000, less than a fifth of the average prewar level (see Table 3.1), and the annual quota for each nation was set at 2 percent of the foreign-born of that nationality recorded by the 1890 Census. The choice of 1890 as the base year placed immigrants from southern and eastern Europe at a still greater disadvantage because few had come to the United States that early. The annual quotas for Italians, Greeks, Slavs, and others from that part of the world represented a mere 3 percent of their prewar annual immigration average. The Immigration Act of 1924 also barred from entry all aliens ineligible for citizenship—that is, it

Table 3.1. The effects of the quota acts on the volume and sources of immigration.

Annual immigration	Immigrants from northern and western Europe	Other immigrants, chiefly from southern and eastern Europe
Average, 1907–1914	176,983	685,531
Under 1921 act	198,082	158,367
Under 1924 act	140,999	20,847
Under national-origins system[a]	127,266	23,235[b]

Source: Based on the annual reports of the Immigration and Naturalization Service.

a. The legal maximum of 150,000 has been exceeded slightly because the legal minimum per-country quota of 100 was in some cases a higher number than the strict application of the national origins formula would have allowed.

b. Southern and eastern Europeans only.

reaffirmed Chinese exclusion and banned many Asians who were declared racially ineligible. For example, the Japanese who had been made racially ineligible for citizenship by a 1922 U.S. Supreme Court ruling were now prohibited from immigrating. Secretary of State Charles Evans Hughes vigorously protested Japanese exclusion because it violated the terms of the 1907–1908 Gentlemen's Agreement, but his protests were ignored.

All immigrants now had to procure a visa from an American consul in their country of origin, a system that provided an opportunity for initial screening, since the thrust of the 1924 act was not only to limit the number of immigrants, but also to select those considered best suited to American society.

Senator Johnson summed up the case for restriction and invoked its broad basis of popular support. The American people, he said,

> have seen, patent and plain, the encroachments of the foreign-born flood upon their own lives. They have come to realize that such a flood, affecting as it does every individual of whatever race or origin, cannot fail likewise to affect the institutions which have made and preserved American liberties. It is no wonder, therefore, that the myth of the melting pot has been discredited. It is no wonder that Americans everywhere are insisting that their land no longer shall offer free and unrestricted asylum to the rest of the world . . .
>
> The United States is our land. If it was not the land of our fathers, at least it may be, and it should be, the land of our children. We intend to maintain it so. The day of unalloyed welcome to all peoples, the day of indiscriminate acceptance of all races, has definitely ended.

Finally, the Immigration Act of 1924 provided for a "national origins" system favoring northern and western European groups which was to replace the formal quota system in 1927. The foundation of restrictionist policy until 1965, the national origins system was designed to prevent further changes in the ethnic composition of American society that might come from a new infusion of immigrants. The total annual immigrant quota from all nations was fixed at 150,000; each country received the percentage of that number that was equal to the percentage of people in the U.S. population of 1920 who could be counted as having derived from that country by birth or descent. A minimum quota of 100 was allotted to every nation, but aliens ineligible for citizenship were barred from access even to these quotas; thus China and Japan theoretically received quotas of 100 each, but in practice the Chinese and Japanese people could not take advantage of them.

Since the U.S. Census did not classify Americans by descent beyond the second generation, national origins were determined by classifying and then counting surnames and by an intricate statistical analysis of the population since 1790 that was crudely adjusted for natural increase. For example, the surname "Smith" was assumed to indicate English ancestry, although it could as well be an Anglicized version of "Schmidt" or could belong to a black person. This dubious procedure gave Great Britain 57 percent of the total annual quota, whereas by using the 1890 Census, Britain would have received only 21 percent. Protests from Scandinavia and German-American civic groups caused the British figure to be recalculated and lowered in favor of other northern and western European countries, whose quotas were thus slightly increased. In the end, northern and western Europe (including the British Isles) received 82 percent of the total annual quota, southern and eastern Europe 16 percent, with 2 percent left to the remaining quota-receiving nations.

Whether the quota system was based on national origins or on the U.S. Census, however, it had the same conceptual weakness. The effort to assign quotas to encourage "assimilable" groups was thwarted by the ethnic diversity of the political units upon which apportioned quotas were based. Both systems assigned quotas to sovereign countries, ignoring the reality that within common political borders a variety of groups might dwell—Czechs, Poles, and others born in Germany, for example, were eligible for entry under the German quota—and that those boundaries might also change; for instance, as Poland's boundaries expanded and contracted, Austrian, Russian, German, and Baltic nationals sometimes qualified, and sometimes did not, under Poland's national quota.

By 1929 the national origins quota system was fully operative. But almost simultaneously immigration to the United States began to drop with the onset of the Great Depression and the series of events that led to World War II, and large portions of most quotas went unfilled. As unemployment rose in 1930, consular officials, acting on instructions from President Herbert Hoover, began vigorously to apply the clause excluding those likely to become public charges, so that all but the relatively well-to-do were prevented from obtaining visas. President Franklin D. Roosevelt subsequently revoked this order (1936), but the failure of the 1924 law to distinguish between immigrants and refugees in tallying annual quota counts still effectively limited the entry of Jewish émigrés who were then fleeing the fascist regimes in Europe. As a result, between 1933 and 1944 fewer than 250,000 refugees were admitted as immigrants, many of them on a nonquota basis. In that period, popularly regarded as the time of refugee immigration, the United States in fact received the smallest influx of newcomers since the 1830s. For the first time in its history, in the 1930s the number of people leaving the United States exceeded the number entering.

By the end of the thirties, when war again appeared imminent, the federal government modified its immigration policy to meet what it defined as the security and defense needs of the nation. A 1941 law (the Smith Act) authorized American consuls to refuse visas to applicants who might endanger "the public safety" and empowered the president to deport any alien whose departure was "in the interest of the United States." The quest for Allied unity during the war resulted in a reversal of the government's hitherto restrictive policy toward the Chinese. On December 17, 1943, Congress repealed the Chinese Exclusion Act dating from 1882 and opened up citizenship to foreign-born Chinese. The salutary effects of the new law were in practice meager, however: the Chinese received only a token quota of 105 and remained the one exception to the policy that continued to exclude all other Asians.

The plight of millions of European refugees, uprooted by the ravages of the war, prompted the federal government to devise measures to help them migrate to the United States. Policy makers became concerned with this issue, in part from efforts to develop better relations with European national groups who might otherwise fall under Soviet influence. President Harry S. Truman issued an executive order in 1945 calling for the admission of 40,000 displaced persons to the United States, to be given priority under the regular quota system. In a more far-reaching move Congress passed the War Brides Act of 1946, which admitted on a nonquota basis some 120,000 alien wives and children and a few hundred husbands of armed-services personnel into the United States. Congress extended similar provisions to Chinese and Japanese spouses in 1947.

The first Displaced Persons Act (1948) provided for the admission for permanent settlement of more than 220,000 people over a two-year period, giving priority to applicants from the Baltic states and setting such an early date to qualify as a displaced person that Jewish and Catholic refugees from Poland, who came later, were largely excluded. Thirty percent of those admitted had to be farmers. Displaced persons were required to have sponsors who would guarantee their housing and employment; security screening was strictly mandated. The most controversial provision of the law—and a victory for moderate restrictionists—was the requirement that displaced persons were not to be admitted as nonquota immigrants. Instead, regular immigration quotas were to be "mortgaged" at 50 percent each year for as many years as it took to "pay back" the displaced persons allowed to enter under its terms. President Truman reluctantly signed the bill, but he found it "flagrantly discriminatory," criticized its restrictive clauses, especially the early cut-off date that "discriminated in callous fashion" against Jews and Catholics, and called for speedy and just amendment.

A revised Displaced Persons Act was passed in 1950 which liberalized the terms of admission and increased the annual quotas: the Baltic and agricultural preferences were removed and the technical provisions discriminating against Jews and Catholics eliminated. Other refugees created by the war's aftermath, such as Greeks and national minorities living inside German borders, were also given quotas. A new ceiling of 415,000 was set for a two-year period, but sponsorship requirements remained, and the mortgaging principle was retained. The latter was dropped in the Refugee Relief Act of 1953, which admitted 205,000 refugees as nonquota immigrants.

The refugee acts showed that the exigencies of winning allies in the Cold War, combined with genuine humanitarian impulses, could loosen overall immigration policy. Annual quota limits were suspended, and in 1956 Congress allowed 20,000 refugees, mainly Hungarians, but also Chinese and Yugoslavs, to immigrate. In 1957 Dutch Indonesian refugees were admitted; in 1960 the World Refugee Year Law admitted displaced persons from Cuba and China. These were among the precedents for the recent program for the resettlement of refugees from Southeast Asia.

The Cold War also had its other side, however, bringing with it the Internal Security Act of 1950, which required the exclusion or deportation of all aliens who had been Communist party members or had belonged to so-called front organizations. National security was also given as the reason behind the need for a reevaluation of the whole body of immigration law. Both restrictionists and those wanting a more open policy agreed that the statutes passed in the early 20th century had to be recodified and updated.

In 1952 Congress approved the Immigration and Nationality (McCarran-Walter) Act, which assembled in a unified
code all previous legislation that had been developed hap-
hazardly for the past century and retained the exclusionary
principle of national origins in fixing quotas. Once more,
Congress had occasion to pass a restrictive immigration act
over a presidential veto, as President Truman refused to sign
the bill. Under the provisions of the McCarran-Walter Act,
northern and western European nations received no less
than 85 percent of the total annual quota. Tighter restrictions
were placed on immigrants from the colonies of quota-receiving countries: their inhabitants could no longer qualify
for admission under the quotas of the mother countries but
were confined to a quota that was set for each colonial territory (a provision designed to cut the flow of black immigrants from the British West Indies, who had previously entered under the ample British quota).

Although the McCarran-Walter Act reaffirmed the old
principle of national origins in its quotas, it abolished the
category of aliens ineligible for citizenship and thereby
loosened restrictions on immigration by Asians: Japan was
given a quota of 185; China retained its quota of 105; and
countries in an area designated the Asia-Pacific Triangle, including colonial areas such as Hong Kong, were given a
quota of 100 each. Although these were small, token quotas,
which lumped these people together with other "undesirable" groups, the practice of excluding Asian races and the
ban on the naturalization of foreign-born Asians were at
least ended.

The McCarran-Walter Act contained other liberalizing features. Special-preference categories were introduced into
each quota for immigrants with extraordinary educational or
technical training or other special abilities. The bill retained
and enlarged the nonquota class, which included immediate
relatives of citizens and of permanent-resident aliens. Thousands of wives from Europe and Asia were able to join their
husbands in the United States. A measure of equal treatment

of the sexes was obtained by the granting of nonquota status to alien husbands of American wives.

In the late 1950s the national origins quota system was beginning to look more and more incompatible with mid-century international relations. The practice of restricting certain national groups had been eroded by refugee acts, the more liberal provisions of the McCarran-Walter Act, and, more generally, by changing public attitudes toward foreign peoples. The system seemed incongruous as the United States proclaimed itself the leader of the "free world" and emphasized its traditional role as an asylum for the oppressed. President John F. Kennedy attacked the system in 1963, charging that it had no "basis in either logic or reason. It neither satisfies a national need nor accomplishes an international purpose." After Kennedy's death, President Lyndon B. Johnson urged Congress to reform it.

The Era of Liberalization, 1965 to the Present

The movement to reform immigration policy culminated in the Hart-Celler Act of 1965 whose provisions took effect in 1968. Both cornerstones of restrictionist policy—the national origins quota system and the designation of the Asia-Pacific Triangle—were abolished. The ceiling on total annual immigration was raised to 290,000. The other countries of the Western Hemisphere had available 120,000 visas annually without limit for any one country; the Eastern Hemisphere had 170,000, of which no one country could use more than 20,000. Applicants were to be admitted on a first-come, first-served basis.

Nonquota admissions were retained in the 1965 act, as was the preferential treatment for certain quota immigrants, especially family members and individuals with particular skills, from the Eastern Hemisphere. No preferential system was provided for the Western Hemisphere. Refugees from both hemispheres were allotted only a small number of visas, but the new law allowed them to be admitted under parole with no numerical limitations.

The act of 1965 increased immigration from countries whose quota allocations had previously placed them at a disadvantage. In the decade before the Hart-Celler Act, China had sent a quota and nonquota total of 1,000 immigrants per year; in 1975 9,000 Chinese immigrants arrived. In 1965 India, Greece, and Portugal supplied 300 immigrants, 4,400 immigrants, and 2,200 immigrants, respectively; by 1975 these numbers had increased to 14,000; 9,800; and 11,000, respectively. Between 1920 and 1960, of all U.S. immigration, Europe as a whole accounted for 60 percent, South and Central America for 35 percent, and Asia for 3 percent. In 1975 Europe accounted for 19 percent, South and Central America for 43 percent, and Asia for 34 percent.

The lack of a preferential-treatment system for the Western Hemisphere nations was a source of complaint. Some immigrants seeking to join relatives who had already immigrated often had to wait a year or two before their numbers came up in the processing pattern that enabled their admission. A solution was reached in the Western Hemisphere Act of 1976 which distributed preferences equally to Eastern and Western Hemisphere nations, and gave Western Hemisphere immigrants with special training, family ties, and skills priority over other immigrants. The 20,000-visa limit for countries in the Eastern Hemisphere was henceforth also applied to the West.

In recent years illegal immigration to the United States has become a controversial policy issue. The number of illegal aliens in the United States is unknown; estimates range between 1 and 8 million. The U.S. Immigration and Naturalization Service reports that it arrests and deports 500,000 people each year, most of them Mexican farm laborers and other unskilled workers. Advocates of restriction argue that these illegal immigrants are taking jobs from both American citizens and legally resident aliens; opponents maintain that they represent a useful supply of unskilled labor willing to perform tasks at low wages that no one else wants to do. Congressmen have sponsored legislation that would make willful employment of illegal aliens unlawful and punishable by imprisonment, but as of 1980 no implementing laws have been passed.

Since the colonial period American immigration policy has been determined by a variety of public institutions and governmental bodies—local until the late 19th century, and thereafter federal—as a result of a movement toward greater centralization of public policy. When the federal government assumed control over immigration, it began to establish criteria for admissions. Restrictive measures were installed and systematically enforced to ensure that only limited numbers and only those foreigners found acceptable by American society would be given entry. In the mid-20th century these exclusionary measures were gradually dismantled; the requirements of a diplomacy based on a closer international order and a growing tolerance for ethnic diversity eventually opened immigration on an equal basis to all national groups.

4

NATURALIZATION AND CITIZENSHIP

Throughout the history of the United States, immigrants, blacks, American Indians, and the inhabitants of U.S. territories have been granted or denied citizenship on the basis of complicated and often contradictory legal standards and administrative procedures. At times their status before the government and the Constitution has been unequal, arbitrary, and poorly defined. To follow the historical development of United States citizenship is to follow the evolution of constitutional principles as they have shaped the boundaries of government power and individual rights, and also to follow the shifting social composition of the nation. The laws of naturalization and, later, of denaturalization would determine which aliens would be allowed to become citizens of the republic.

As the laws defining citizenship and naturalization grew more precise and more rigorously administered, a clearer conception of American nationality emerged and citizens' obligations to the federal government were prescribed more exactly. Lawmakers in the 19th century enlarged the scope of the legal and constitutional rights of U.S. citizenship and, in the 20th century, used a common citizenship and a popular naturalization process to fuse diverse ethnic groups into one nation.

The Colonial Period, 1600–1775

In American society admission to the political community as a citizen involves a voluntary pledge of allegiance and an agreement to follow the laws of the country's sovereign government. In return, the government confers legal, constitutional status and political privileges on its citizens. Citizenship can be acquired by *jus soli* (birth within the borders of the United States or its possessions), by *jus sanguinis* (the inheritance of the nationality of the parents), or through the process of naturalization. Citizenship by *jus soli* or *jus sanguinis* is assumed to include the same allegiance to the government as that sworn in solemn oath when a person becomes a naturalized citizen.

Citizenship in the United States has its origin in the laws of subjectship of 16th-century England, which were in turn based on feudal notions regarding natural laws governing the rulers and the ruled. Subjectship was an essential element in the natural order of the world that was perpetual and unchanging. The tie between the state and its citizens was exemplified by the bond between the king and his subject, a relationship that was itself derived from the natural principle of subjection and dominance obtaining between parent and child. The king supplied protection to the subjects, who gave service, allegiance, and obedience in return. These reciprocal duties were indissoluble; no willful act on either side could break the ties that bound them together.

Although the idea of immutable subjectship long remained in England's constitutional law, it was influenced by new social pressures in the North American colonies. In the 17th and 18th centuries an acute need for men to till the new land opened these colonies up to newcomers from the European continent and the British Isles. English law provided for the naturalization of foreigners, and it was presumed to provide for aliens settling in the New World colonies as well, but unforeseen problems and circumstances soon arose everywhere. Colonial governments, proprietors, the Crown,

and Parliament vied with each other to control the procedures for bestowing subjectship on the foreign peoples
streaming into the new land. The traditional English legal
strictures against property ownership and commercial enterprise by aliens seemed inappropriate in colonies where land
was abundant and the economy underdeveloped, but to
what sovereign power would these aliens—or native-born
Englishmen, for that matter—owe their primary allegiance
and loyalty? Would it be the colonial assembly, the Parliament, or the king?

Since under English law only the Crown and Parliament
possessed the power to turn foreigners into British subjects,
English jurists and Parliament ruled out the idea that colonial governments could perform that function for alien settlers. Aliens residing in the colonies who sought equal civil
status with English subjects had to petition the king or Parliament for special naturalization, even though from the earliest days colonies such as Virginia and New York had naturalized alien newcomers. Since full civil status, political
rights, and the economic privileges of the English-born
could only be obtained through the imperial government,
the French Huguenots, Walloons, and other immigrants of
the period frequently paused in London to secure English
subjectship before moving on to North America.

Parliamentary standards for the naturalization of foreigners were usually based on religious tests. In 1609 Parliament
passed a sacramental-test act that excluded Catholics from
eligibility for special parliamentary grants of subjectship,
along with Jews and other non-Christian groups. The
Crown, however, did not observe these religious restrictions
in granting naturalization. After the Puritan revolution and
the restoration of the monarchy, Charles II and James II prac-
ticed a generous policy of granting individual "letters patent
of denization" to Jews and Catholics, and exempted the recipients from the routine alien customs charges. Jews also
received extensive commercial and trade privileges from the
Crown, which local authorities were not empowered to confer. When Charles II opened the dominions of the British

Empire to the French Huguenot refugees driven out of France by French royal policy and promised them royal denization, hundreds of refugees flocked to England and eventually to the North American colonies. A French Huguenot refugee in Boston counseled other immigrants to "become naturalized in London, in order to be at liberty to engage in traffic of all kinds, and to voyage among the English Islands; without this, it cannot be done." As Protestants, the Huguenots, unlike Jews and Catholics, could obtain naturalization by special act of Parliament, as well as by denization through royal letters patent.

Throughout the 17th century, Parliament resisted the Crown's requests for the establishment of a general naturalization law. It was apprehensive about competition from foreigners who would then be permitted to enter British trade. Religious intolerance and fears of foreign subversion also convinced Parliament to maintain a restrictive immigration policy.

At the beginning of the 18th century, partisan attitudes toward the issue of admitting aliens into the empire reflected the split between the Whig and Tory parties in England. The Whigs accused the "average Tory squire" of "unabashed insularity" that nourished the "belief that Whiggery itself and all it stood for was an alien growth, which would wither without the nurture it received from foreign sources." The Whigs themselves, in contrast, welcomed "the injection of foreign capital and enterprise into the English economy which Protestant refugees had already provided." They supported a general policy that would speed the development of the imperial colonies by settling industrious foreigners, and many were in favor of a more convenient naturalization law. Colonial governments and colonists, long hampered by the lack of such a law, had asked for a parliamentary grant that would empower colonial governments to naturalize foreigners. To alien and English-born colonists alike, the administration in London of the naturalization process was an inconvenience.

A turning point in English policy was almost reached in

1709 when the Whigs gained a clear majority in Parliament and passed an act that provided a simple procedure for the naturalization of foreigners. Aliens had only to swear allegiance to, and acknowledge the supremacy of, the Crown, prove that they had received a Protestant sacrament in the preceding three months, and declare in open court against the doctrine of transubstantiation. Those who could satisfy these conditions were granted the same rights and status as natural-born subjects. The fee was one shilling.

This act remained in force only three years, but even in that brief time many foreign Protestants were naturalized under its terms. Some of them, such as the German refugees from the Palatinate, eventually made their way to the American colonies. After its repeal in 1712, aliens seeking to become British subjects had once again to petition Parliament or obtain denization by royal decree.

Not until 1740 did Parliament finally enact a general naturalization law permitting foreigners in America to acquire subjectship locally. Under this law, applicants had to be residents in "any of His Majesty's Colonies in America" for at least seven years without being absent for more than two consecutive months, had to present a certificate signed by two witnesses corroborating that in the previous three months they had taken the sacrament "in some Protestant and Reformed Congregation," and had to swear allegiance to the king and profess Christian belief before a colonial judge in open court. Quakers and Jews were exempted from the sacramental requirement and could swear oaths in keeping with their beliefs, but the law prohibited the naturalization of Catholics. Its most important innovation was the proviso that the rights of a person naturalized under its terms were to be honored in every dominion of the empire.

The last major British naturalization law affecting American colonists was an act of 1761 that enabled the British army to naturalize foreign Protestants who had served, or would serve, for two years in the British military in the colonies, provided they swore the necessary oaths and had received a Protestant sacrament in the preceding six months. The imperial apparatus for administering general naturalization was complete, and it was a model of enlightened toleration. Aliens naturalized under the laws of 1740 and 1761 received the same civil and political status as natural-born subjects: they could engage in trade, gain title to land, vote, and hold office.

The colonists, however, were not satisfied. From the beginning of settlement the feeling had grown that the colonies should have some authority over the admission of new members. Eager to lure settlers to develop the land, the Americans sought to establish an easy and generous naturalization policy. In the century before the 1740 law, colonists had experimented with local awards of denization. Virginia and the Carolinas established a system of naturalization through individual enrollment regulated in local courts. In New England towns, aliens were naturalized when they were admitted to freemen's status. In other colonies, proprietors and royal governors bestowed letters patent of denization, and several colonial legislatures issued special and general naturalization acts. In 1682 Pennsylvania naturalized "Strangers and Foreigners" inhabiting the lower counties of Jones, Newcastle, and Whoreskill who swore allegiance to the king and the proprietor within three months of arrival; it charged a fee of 20 shillings. In 1683 New York also naturalized all resident foreigners "professing Christianity" by administering an oath of allegiance.

The imperial government was slow to react to these colonial gestures: an order in the Privy Council did not officially terminate the practice of colonial awards of subjectship until 1700. Even then, the order allowed denization by the acts of colonial assemblies to continue so long as the new subjects received a civil status valid only in the colony granting naturalization. Colonial governments continued to pass their own naturalization laws until 1773, when the practice was permanently proscribed.

Although the naturalization laws of 1740 and 1761 provided the universal status of British subject, as opposed to the purely local subjectship granted by the colonies, and in spite of fees much higher than the two shillings charged by agents administering the imperial statute, masses of foreign immigrants continued to apply to colonial governments for naturalization, possibly because they did not care to risk waiting the seven years required for subjectship by imperial law.

The abolition of the colonial naturalization acts was part of a wider movement by the Crown and Parliament toward greater administrative control over the colonies of the empire. In 1764 the imperial government contended that foreigners who had not been naturalized under the law of 1740 had no rights of property ownership. In 1773, after Pennsylvania and New Jersey had passed new naturalization acts, the Crown nullified the acts and instructed all colonial governors to prohibit the passing of any more local naturalization laws. To the shocked colonists this unprecedented restriction appeared as part of a sinister design to deprive them of their rights and privileges as English subjects. In the Declaration of Independence they charged George III with a tyrannical attempt to "prevent the population of these states; for that purpose obstructing the laws for the naturalization of foreigners," which, along with other grievances, gave the colonists a warrant to sever their political ties with England forever and to establish new republican governments.

Having thus freed themselves to give their allegiance to another government, the colonies formulated a new theory of contractual allegiance. It had its roots in the political ideas of the Enlightenment, particularly of the English philosopher John Locke, reinforced by a century of colonial practice that had altered the English concept of naturalization and allegiance. Since naturalization had been central to the process of forming colonial societies, the colonists began to see political allegiance as reflecting the essential character of naturalization itself and to hold that allegiance was volitional and contractual.

During the Revolution and the formation of an American

government that followed, colonial statesmen recast the tradition of British subjectship. They rejected the concept that subjectship was unchanging and perpetual, asserting instead that any legitimate government rested on the principle of majority rule for which "*individual assent* is necessary, or it deserves the name of usurpation, and ought to be execrated as tyranny." Requiring the assent of the governed enabled the colonists to exchange subjectship under the British king for citizenship in the American republic. Under the new state and federal governments, every man was theoretically free to choose to be citizen or alien; his civil status was defined by an act of individual will. As a practical expedient to legitimize consent, the Continental Congress in 1776 affirmed that simply residing in a state and receiving its legal protection constituted allegiance to the new political order.

The New Republic, 1776–1850

After the outbreak of the American Revolution, the new state governments quickly assumed control of naturalization policy by legislative acts, constitutional provision, and the simple exercise of executive power. New York, Pennsylvania, North Carolina, and Vermont established uniform rules for naturalization in their respective constitutions. The legislatures of Maryland, South Carolina, Virginia, and Georgia passed laws prescribing the conditions and procedures of acquiring state citizenship. South Carolina preserved the feature of graded citizenship contained in the British law of subjectship. "Free white persons" who had resided in South Carolina for one year and who swore allegiance to the state government were recognized as citizens, but they could acquire voting rights for the assembly and the city corporation of Charleston only after another year of residency; they could not be candidates for political office until they had received a special naturalization grant from the state assembly.

Although each state in the American nation developed different laws and administrative procedures for naturalization, they had a set of basic conditions in common. All required the applicant to take a public oath of allegiance to the state government. States that had passed general naturalization acts required that those persons applying for citizenship demonstrate good character through personal references, certificates, or witnesses, and nearly every state had some specified period of residency required before political privileges were granted. All states asked applicants to publicly disavow allegiance to any foreign sovereign.

The national government created by the Articles of Confederation was guided by the conviction that federal powers must be sharply delimited. The Articles gave Congress no control over naturalization or the rights of citizenship, though they did specify that each state must honor the basic civil rights of citizens of other states. The free inhabitants of a state were entitled to all privileges and immunities of citizens in the others and were permitted to come and go among them as they pleased. This clause soon stirred resentment and controversy in certain quarters. Some states complained that they were being deluged by "obnoxious aliens" who had to be given the full rights of citizenship simply because they had been naturalized by another state. James Madison urged that the Continental Congress set a uniform standard for citizenship in order to put an end to disputes among the states over naturalization policy, and eventually several states did submit plans for federal control of citizenship and naturalization to the Constitutional Convention of 1787.

All the delegates to that convention agreed that the new Constitution should empower the federal government to establish a uniform rule of naturalization. The grant of authority they designed was intended not only to produce a national standard consistent with the Constitution's comity clause, which continued the confederation's controversial principle of interstate citizenship, but to ensure that state governments would never abuse their naturalization power. The federal government's power over naturalization was construed as the authority to remove the disabilities of foreign birth, but the Constitution left to the states the authority to establish the positive rights and privileges of naturalized citizenship. As a further concession to state autonomy, it also assumed that federal or national citizenship would automatically derive from the acquisition of state citizenship.

Another critical issue dealt with at the Philadelphia convention was whether the British tradition of graded civil status should be reproduced in the United States. The need for settlers had early forced the colonists to make the terms for naturalization easy, and those generously offered rights had long since blurred the distinctions between the various legal ranks of subjects found in English law. Some delegates, including Madison, suggested a plan by which applicants would receive incremental rights as, step by step, they fulfilled the basic requirements of citizenship. They also debated limiting the vote and membership in Congress to the native-born. In the end, however, the convention agreed that the only disadvantage to be placed upon naturalized citizens would be ineligibility for the presidency of the United States. As finally drafted, the Constitution repudiated graded citizenship as well as any notion that native-born and naturalized citizens should possess different sets of rights, and confirmed the principle that U.S. citizenship, once conferred, would be uniform and complete.

Despite these clear principles, the Constitution contained ambiguities and potential areas for dispute over the nature of citizenship. It failed, for example, to define precisely what the rights and obligations of national citizenship were to be, nor did it adequately define the relationship between state and federal citizenship. The Bill of Rights added further confusion by referring to the rights of the "people," rather than of citizens. In the 19th century the Constitution's silence on these subjects posed problems in the formulation of a legal code defining the civil position of free blacks.

The framework for the naturalization process was erected in a series of statutes passed in the 1790s. The first federal naturalization law in 1790 required that an applicant be a "free white person" who had resided for two years "within the limits and under the jurisdiction of the United States." The law also granted jurisdiction over naturalization to "any common law court of record in any one of the states." To undercut the political support that aliens tended to give the Jeffersonians, the Federalist party secured the passage of a law in 1795 that raised the residency requirement for naturalization from 2 to 5 years and in 1798 to 14. When the Jeffersonian Republicans came to power in 1801, they set the basic residency requirement back to 5 years, where it has remained ever since.

The ambiguous legal position in which inhabitants of the new western territories found themselves raised the first serious question about the relation of federal to local citizenship. The Northwest Ordinance of 1787, which had established the Northwest Territories, had said nothing about the naturalization of their inhabitants. Those migrants who came from the established states farther east were still U.S. citizens in the territories by virtue of their state-derived local citizenship, though they had relinquished their state citizenship by emigration. But those newcomers who immigrated directly from a foreign country had no citizenship at all and no way of acquiring it. To provide some legal civil status for those territorial inhabitants, the Senate in 1795 gave territorial courts the authority to naturalize foreigners. Both the native-born and the naturalized residents of territories remained without state citizenship.

The civil status of American Indians was also long a source of perplexity, but in the early 19th century Indian civil-rights cases followed a trend that eventually defined their legal position. Through a gradual accumulation of judicial opinions, each Indian tribal organization came to be regarded as a "nation" to whom Indians owed their primary allegiance; thus the courts designated Indians noncitizens because, although they were born in U.S. territory, their allegiance remained to the tribe.

The first great wave of immigrants following the establishment of the republic began to arrive shortly after the War of 1812. Many of these new settlers were eager to become citizens. The law of 1802 required that applicants be free white persons and that they declare their intention of becoming citizens at least three years prior to naturalization. They could file their applications at any local court of record; they had to be residents for five years in the United States and one year in the state to which they applied; finally, they had to swear an oath to uphold the Constitution and renounce allegiance to any foreign sovereign. In accordance with the common-law doctrine of the primacy of male citizenship, a wife and any children under 21 years of age became citizens at the time of the husband's own naturalization. These provisions were amended by Congress in 1824 to accelerate the naturalization process. The minimum time between the declaration of intention and the final award of citizenship papers was shortened to two years, and anyone residing in the country for the three years preceding the age of majority was allowed to take out both papers at once.

The easy terms for naturalization under federal statute were paralleled by the generous state laws and state constitutions of the 19th century that conferred political, commercial, and property rights on aliens. A uniform national rule for acquiring citizenship existed, but the states were left free to fix the political and civil rights of aliens. Western states, for example, manipulated the franchise to attract immigrants and absorb them into local life. In 1846 Wisconsin permitted all aliens who had filed a declaration of intention and who had resided in the state for one year to vote. Michigan in 1850 granted the right to vote to aliens who had been residents for two and a half years. Several states allowed nearly complete citizenship rights to any person who had filed a declaration of intention and who had resided in the state for a short period. All state and territorial governments placed either minimal or no restrictions on property-holding or commercial enterprise by aliens.

Natives who were eagerly promoting the development of the country, and aliens who had recently settled there, both pressured Congress to ease the federal requirements for citizenship. Citizens from New Jersey and New York urged Congress in 1824 to relax the probationary laws for naturalization. "Sundry aliens of Louisiana" asked Congress in the same year to enact federal naturalization laws that would make acquiring citizenship easier, while "sundry citizens of New York state" similarly petitioned the House of Representatives in 1835 to eliminate the declaration of intention and give aliens all the privileges of citizenship after only two years of residence.

Naturalization proceedings in the 19th century were extremely loose and casually administered. In a congressional report submitted to the Senate in 1845, based on investigations of naturalization proceedings in New York City, Philadelphia, and Baltimore, a judge of the marine court in the southern district of New York testified that only one witness was required to vouch for the character of an applicant and that the witness was never cross-examined. The judge also suspected that many of the people testifying on behalf of applicants were hired witnesses. Another justice of the marine court stated that a person could easily get several duplicate certificates of his declaration of intention which he would then distribute or sell at election time. The congressional report also described how in the New York Superior Court applicants were sworn in en masse, and their papers automatically approved. Tammany Hall organized committees that filled out application forms and affidavits for aliens and paid the required naturalization fees. The congressional report showed that the state courts, where fees were lower and standards less rigorous, naturalized many more applicants than the federal courts did. In New York City, Philadelphia, and Baltimore, naturalization rates rose sharply during the two weeks preceding each spring and fall election.

In opposition to this liberal policy toward aliens in the mid-19th century, the Know-Nothing party—a nativist political movement that rose spectacularly in the early 1850s only to vanish just as rapidly—called for legislation curtailing alien political and civil rights. Obsessed with the notion that Catholic immigrants were taking over the country, the Know-Nothings petitioned Congress on several occasions to reform the naturalization law, extend the residency requirement, and exclude Roman Catholics from public office. The party controlled the Massachusetts legislature from 1854 to 1856 and was strong in several other states, but the Know-Nothings were unable to secure the 21-year residency requirement they sought for state citizenship, and in spite of their efforts the road to naturalization remained unobstructed.

Sectional Crisis and Reconstruction, 1851–1890

In the first half of the 19th century, the constitutional and legal definition of American citizenship became a critical issue, as the controversy over the relation between state- and federal-government powers began to focus on the relationship between state and federal citizenship. Throughout the first half of the century, lawmakers and judges avoided making clear distinctions between the two, aware that every decision could have incalculable effects upon the delicate balance between federal and state power.

The absence of the formal distinction between the two citizenships in the Constitution challenged the ingenuity of courts and legislatures. As the nation expanded westward and newly formed states petitioned to enter the Union, the state-federal relationship became an explosive issue. The congressional debate over the admission of Missouri to the Union in 1820, which involved the future status of free blacks in Missouri, brought the matter to a head.

The issue arose over a provision in the Missouri constitution that prohibited free blacks and mulattoes from entering the state. Congressmen from the northern states contended that this provision violated the comity clause of the Constitution which bound each state to honor citizenship conferred by any other. Southern representatives repudiated this view on the grounds that free blacks were simply not citizens. In the Senate, James Burrill of Rhode Island and David L. Morril of New Hampshire pointed out that free blacks had acquired federal citizenship by satisfying the conditions prescribed by the states where they resided. Morril warned that if any state were allowed to discriminate arbitrarily against the citizens created by another state, the unraveling of federal bonds would inevitably follow. In opposing Morril, southern congressmen asserted that the rights of citizenship were derived from the municipal authority of each state; they were wholly local in their origins and, consequently, in their validity; they bestowed no right to federal immunities and privileges. Some legislators, such as Louis McLane of Delaware, held that no blacks would conform to "that description of persons contemplated by the Constitution of the United States as entitled to federal rights."

After months of debate, Congress finally admitted Missouri to the Union as a slave state, and ratified Missouri's constitution on the condition that the disputed provision could not exclude "any citizen of either of the States in this Union . . . from the enjoyment of any of the privileges and immunities to which such citizen is entitled under the Constitution of the United States," but it ignored the central issue of citizenship for free blacks and mulattoes. The debate over the admission of Missouri had split the nation, laying bare the irreconcilable ideas about the character of citizenship held by free and slave states that would be elaborated in the ensuing decades.

Southern states foresaw the undermining of their fundamental right to determine whom they would recognize as equal members of civil society. As the nonslave states that were formed out of the western territories began to admit free blacks to citizenship, the South was compelled to challenge the assumption that federal citizenship flowed from state citizenship. If southerners could not prove that state citizenship was purely local in effect and that the framers of the Constitution never intended blacks to be citizens, they faced the necessity of yielding the full rights of citizenship to free blacks—an eventuality that could lead to fundamental questions about the legal status and rights of slaves. A judge in Mississippi summed up the southern position: the state of Ohio might "confer citizenship on the chimpanzee or ourangoutang," he quipped sardonically, but no comity clause or legal, constitutional technicality could compel "states not thus demented to forget their own policy . . . and lower their own citizens."

Virginia and South Carolina were the first of several southern states to establish laws prohibiting free blacks from entering their jurisdiction, and Florida placed a clause in its state constitution of 1845 that banned their entry. Some federal officials held that those exclusionary laws violated free commerce between the states as well as the comity clause. But many, including Andrew Jackson's attorney general, John Berrien, argued that such laws were a legitimate exercise of a state's municipal police power. Congress continually debated their legality, but most of them remained in force up to the Civil War.

The Dred Scott case of 1857 produced a Supreme Court decision that heightened the legal confusion and sectional controversy over the constitutional definition of citizenship. Dred Scott was a Missouri slave who had resided in the free state of Illinois and the free territory of Minnesota, and sued for his freedom on the grounds that his residency in a free area had nullified his status as a slave. Chief Justice Roger B. Taney, who wrote the majority opinion for the Court, held that, because Scott was not a citizen of Missouri, he could not bring suit in a federal court to begin with. Furthermore, under the terms of the Constitution, no free black could ever become a citizen of the United States. He invoked the traditional distinction between state and federal citizenship, reaffirming the legal opinion that the latter derived from the former. The framers of the Constitution, he maintained, had never intended freed blacks to be admitted to the political community of citizens. Thus Taney disposed of the contention that blacks who were born free were citizens. He also decided that no black could gain citizenship by naturalization since all the relevant statutes had mentioned only "free whites" as potential candidates. Finally, he concluded that rights granted by individual states did not confer citizenship; instead, the granting of the status of U.S. citizen conferred political and civil rights.

The Dred Scott decision underscored the ambiguities in the constitutional definition of citizenship. It upheld the notion of dual citizenship and in the process left ample room for conflict between federal and state authority in granting citizenship. It failed to determine the relative priorities of allegiance to the state and allegiance to the federal government. Finally, it ignored the need to establish who could and could not claim protection under the Constitution. The concept of citizenship that emerged from the decision reflected the ambiguous structure of political relations undergirding the federal republic. But it also reflected a halting movement toward a narrower definition of American nationality: only the descendants of those who had made the compact to form the republic in 1787 and free white aliens were eligible for citizenship under federal law.

In the first half of the 19th century, jurists and statesmen had shied away from the task of formulating a precise definition of citizenship because it would only have exacerbated growing sectional tensions. The Civil War and Reconstruction, however, brought the opportunity to clarify the relationship between state and federal government and the allegiance owed by citizens to each. The Civil Rights Act of 1866 established in federal law that "all persons born in the United States and not subject to any foreign power, excluding Indians not taxed," would receive United States citizenship. This law breached the legal wall erected by Taney that had restricted birthright citizenship to the children of free white aliens and to descendants of the citizens of the original thirteen states. The Fourteenth Amendment ratified in 1868 went a step further by incorporating the 1866 law into the Constitution. Although local courts had applied the common-law principle of citizenship by place of birth (*jus soli*), the Fourteenth Amendment established it as a national policy. The law of citizenship by the allegiance of parents, *jus sanguinis*, which Taney had invoked in extended form, was henceforth to play a minor role in the laws of naturalization.

Since the Fourteenth Amendment stated that "all persons born or naturalized in the United States, and subject to the jurisdiction thereof, are citizens of the United States and of the state wherein they reside," the allegiance of every citizen to the federal government was spelled out in precise terms. State citizens were perforce United States citizens, and no state could violate the rights of any U.S. citizen: "No state shall make or enforce any law which shall abridge the privileges or immunities of citizens of the United States; nor shall any State deprive any person of life, liberty, or property, without due process of law; nor deny to any person within its jurisdiction the equal protection of the laws." Thus, the Fourteenth Amendment asserted the primacy of federal citizenship and dissolved the former principle that it flowed ultimately from state powers.

In its first judicial review of the Fourteenth Amendment, the Slaughter-House Cases of 1873, the Supreme Court sharply circumscribed the federal government's capacity to define and safeguard the "immunities and privileges of citizens of the United States." In this case, the right of the state of Louisiana to grant an exclusive slaughterhouse franchise to a corporation in New Orleans was upheld; the Court found that the Fourteenth Amendment did not confer to citizens privileges and immunities that they had not possessed before its adoption; that property rights, personal rights, and civil rights were matters to be fixed by state law and state action; and that the federal government could act to safeguard only those rights broadly articulated by the Constitution or that owed their existence to the character of the federal government. The Court declined to prescribe or systematically define the "immunities and privileges" of U.S. citizens; instead, it reluctantly sketched a vague outline of general rights deriving from constitutional principles. The rights of national citizenship thus remained both limited and ambiguous.

Nevertheless, after a half-century of political controversy and civil war, in the era of Reconstruction steps were taken toward establishing the dominance of the Union and the universality of federal citizenship. Radical Republicans tried to unite blacks and whites as equal citizens in a national polity and in doing so to affirm an expansive ideal of American nationality. One of them declared that the nation was "inclusive of the whole people . . . There is no difference of wealth, or race, or physical condition, that can be made the ground of exclusion from it."

Despite the optimism with which some Americans greeted Reconstruction, many policy makers continued to subscribe to a fixed and limited definition of U.S. nationality. During congressional debate on a revised naturalization law in 1870, Senator Charles Sumner of Massachusetts, a leading supporter of Reconstruction, proposed an amendment that would open naturalization to nonwhite as well as white aliens, but the measure was vehemently opposed by the western states, who were by that time intent on excluding alien Chinese from citizenship. Sumner invoked the Declaration of Independence in a Fourth of July oration to argue, "It is 'all men' and not a race or color that are placed under the protection of the Declaration, and such was the voice of our fathers . . . The word 'white' wherever it occurs as a limitation of rights, must disappear. Only in this way can you be consistent with the Declaration."

Sumner's motion was voted down 30 to 14. Shortly after, however, Congress made aliens of African descent or nativity eligible for naturalization. Under that law Arabs and Hindus from Africa, but not necessarily from Asia, could qualify for naturalization, a measure that laid the basis for future problems by mixing geographic with ethnic or racial qualifications for citizenship.

The Fourteenth Amendment assured that U.S. citizens could not be deprived of citizenship in any state, but no such law prevented a state from granting its citizenship to anyone found qualified, even if unqualified for U.S. naturalization, until a series of decisions in lower federal courts closed that possibility. In 1871 the Circuit Court of the Southern District of Alabama held that "citizenship in a state is a result of citizenship in the United States." In 1875 the Circuit Court of Appeals for the District of Minnesota ruled that "when the Constitution . . . says that Congress shall have power 'to establish a uniform rule of naturalization,' it designed these rules . . . to be the *only rules* by which a citizen or subject of a foreign government could become a citizen or subject of one of the states of this union . . . and the United States." In 1893 the same court decided that a foreign-born resident who had not been naturalized according to federal law was a citizen neither of the United States nor of a state. By the late 19th century the federal courts had reached a consensus that there could be no state citizenship without federal citizenship.

New Aliens and New Policies, 1891–1940

Beginning in 1882 a series of laws suspending the entry of Chinese laborers was passed by Congress, introducing a new category into immigration laws. That category was "aliens ineligible for citizenship," and it included all Chinese immigrants. For the first time in the nation's history, a federal law prescribed that an immigrant group of a specified national origin was denied access to U.S. citizenship. Before the passage of the 1882 Chinese Exclusion Act, legislators and jurists had been plagued by the question of whether the Chinese were ineligible because they were nonwhite or because no specific law granted them this privilege.

The federal government assumed control over national immigration policy in 1891, and Congress immediately enacted the first effective law governing the deportation of illegal aliens, a law which the Supreme Court found constitutional on the grounds that deportation was an administrative, not a criminal, proceeding and therefore not subject to the due process of law guaranteed by the Fourteenth Amendment. Although a minority opinion described the deportation as a "severe and cruel" punishment inflicted upon foreigners for "no crime but that of their race and birthplace," federal officials began to establish standard procedures for deportation cases, which included arrest without warrant, detention without warrant, and denial of counsel until proceedings were well advanced. An alien could be subjected to cross-examination to determine whether his case was "inherently improbable," even if administrative officials had no evidence against him. In *Quock Ting* v. *United States* (1891), a Chinese boy who claimed to have lived in the United States for the first ten years of his life was deported because during his interrogation he did not know the names of streets of places in the area in which he claimed to have been brought up. Since the boy knew no English, an interpreter had to be used. The boy's testimony did not meet the criterion of "inherent probability." Officials were enjoined not to disregard the testimony of witnesses on racial grounds, but they were not required to give equal weight to the testimony of different races or nationalities; it was considered legally proper for officials to assume that some races were more apt to tell the truth than others.

In 1892 Congress passed the Geary Act, a comprehensive law that extended the exclusion of Chinese laborers for ten more years, denied bail to Chinese aliens in habeas corpus proceedings, ordered the immediate deportation of illegal Chinese residents, and required that all Chinese laborers carry certificates of residency. Foreign-born Chinese had to register with the Treasury Department and were subject to the police powers of the collector of internal revenue; theoretically, at least, they were placed under constant federal surveillance. They could be asked to show their residency papers at any time, and they were accountable to federal authorities for virtually all their actions.

The assassination in 1901 of President William McKinley by the immigrant anarchist Leon Czolgosz inspired a still more comprehensive deportation law. In 1903 Congress passed a law that made anarchism grounds for deportation, the first federal law to make political belief grounds for expulsion. Becoming a "public charge," and "moral turpitude," if it could be proved, could lead to summary deportation up to two years after arrival.

The Bureau of Immigration and Naturalization was established in 1906 in the Department of Commerce and Labor to administer a new naturalization law: the first major federal act since the law of 1802 that affected the naturalization process. The tangle of procedures and tests used to determine suitability for citizenship was to be codified and administered under the even-handed guidance of bureau chiefs. The naturalization process itself comprised three steps: the filing of a declaration of intention (first papers), the filing of a petition for naturalization under the applicant's signature (second papers), and a hearing on the petition which would grant or deny the certificate of naturalized citizenship (final papers). The declaration had to be submitted no less than two years and no more than seven years before a petition was filed. There was a wait of 90 days between the petition and the hearing to allow time for an investigation and to make the hearing public. The judge cross-examined in English; two witnesses had to vouch for the applicant's "moral character" and "attachment to the principles of the Constitution." The applicant was asked questions on American history and civics, and had to satisfy the court that he was neither an anarchist nor a polygamist, that he had "resided continuously within the United States five years at least, and within the State or Territory where such court is at the time held one year at least." Finally, he had to prove his ability to speak English.

To ensure that the procedures and standards for naturalization would be closely followed, the bureau stationed around the country 300 naturalization examiners supervised by 23 district directors. The federal procedure for naturalization was governed by a large administrative bureaucracy, which, it was hoped, would eliminate the frauds, corruption, and low standards for admission so characteristic of 19th-century proceedings. To discourage the abuse of naturalization for partisan political purposes, the law of 1906 banned any naturalization hearings within 30 days of any general election in a court's area of jurisdiction.

The casual system of naturalization that the state governments had followed before the Civil War was still functioning in the 1870s and 1880s. Local managers in both political parties herded recently arrived immigrants to court to see that they got naturalization papers in time to vote in the next election. Many, particularly in the large eastern cities, voted with fraudulent papers. In the early 1880s, 18 states and territories had granted voting rights to aliens who had only filed a declaration of intention.

Widespread alien suffrage and the lax administration of naturalization laws began to attract the attention of social reformers and nativists alike. They equally deplored immigrant political influence and corruption at the polls by fraud and alien suffrage. Many advocated lengthening the residency requirement; some revived the Know-Nothing demand for a minimum 21-year naturalization period.

By the end of the 19th century the movement to end alien suffrage and to raise the standards for acquiring citizenship had won powerful advocates. In several states, one critic warned, huge numbers of aliens were voting for members of Congress: eventually aliens might elect enough representatives to control the entire Congress. Another reported that in one Nebraska county the great majority of declarations were being made as a direct result of inducements from political campaigners.

The lax enforcement of the law was also discouraging naturalization, since the declaration of intention appeared to be all that one needed to exercise all the rights and privileges of citizenship. In the early 20th century several states heeded the warning that the ballot in the hands of aliens would have disastrous consequences for democracy. By the outbreak of World War I, only seven states had laws permitting alien suffrage, and those were vestiges of constitutions from earlier frontier days.

As the Congress and the courts tightened restrictions on the political activities of aliens, they also began to specify suitability for citizenship in terms of ethnic origins. The large numbers of people immigrating to the United States from the Near and Far East raised thorny problems that had originated with the law that declared the Chinese ineligible for citizenship. The combination of racial prejudice and the native worker's hostility to cheap foreign labor aroused ferocious antagonism toward the Chinese. Added to this was a general conviction that the Chinese would not adopt American habits of egalitarianism and individualism required to participate in a modern, industrializing society. Nativists saw them as unassimilable masses from an ancient and rigid civilization who were incapable of acculturation. The Chinese constantly looked back to their kinsmen, ancestral village, headman, and emperor. Californians complained that they had no interest in adopting American habits, modes of dress, and education; did not understand the sanctity of an oath; and did not even want to become citizens or perform a citizen's duties.

Policy makers struggled to find a consistent means of determining the suitability of the various ethnic groups for citizenship. A rule of thumb for doing so was derived from the amended naturalization law of 1870 which provided that only free whites and aliens of "African descent or African nativity" could apply for citizenship, but exactly what "white" meant now posed problems. In the 1870s legislatures and courts were still confused about which races would be included under the category of eligible white persons: a few Chinese on the East Coast and in western states had been naturalized before the exclusion act of 1882. Another problem was the status of children whose parents were ineligible for citizenship. Although they were obviously of the same disqualified race they had been born in the United States and thus were fully entitled by the Fourteenth Amendment to be considered U.S. citizens, a point that was affirmed by the Supreme Court in the case of the *United States* v. *Wong Kim Ark* (1898). Although the racial criterion of the naturalization law was in fundamental conflict with the Constitution, that problem was conveniently ignored.

Despite the federal law's denial of citizenship to the Chinese and the prescription that only "free whites" and those of African descent could be naturalized, the courts granted citizenship to substantial numbers of Asian immigrants. The U.S. Census of 1910 recorded 1,368 naturalized Chinese, and 420 naturalized Japanese in the United States. Misuji Miyakawa, the chief counsel for the Japanese plaintiffs in the 1906 San Francisco school desegregation case that had led to the Gentlemen's Agreement by which Japan regulated the immigration of its own laborers, was Japanese-born, naturalized, and a member of the California bar.

Judges and legislators were uncertain about the status of the brown-skinned Mexicans, but eventually developed a line of reasoning that allowed them to consider Mexicans eligible for citizenship. In 1897, a U.S. district court in Texas held that they could be classified neither as white nor as being of Asian or of African descent, but that despite their being nonwhite they could be naturalized individually because the constitution of the Republic of Texas and the laws and treaties of the United States had granted collective acts of naturalization to Mexicans when Texas entered the Union.

Because the naturalization statutes were ambiguous, the

courts tended to rely on subjective considerations, popular opinion, and various, often conflicting, criteria to decide which ethnic groups could qualify for naturalization. Eventually the line between eligible and ineligible aliens was drawn by a crude definition of the nonwhite and non-African category. In 1910 the Bureau of Immigration and Naturalization ordered court clerks to reject declarations from aliens who were neither white persons nor persons of African birth or descent. In 1893 a Japanese had been rejected for naturalization because he was nonwhite, but this had been an isolated case. Between 1910 and 1920, however, Japanese applicants were consistently turned down, and finally in 1922 the Supreme Court in *Ozawa* v. *The United States* affirmed that Japanese aliens were nonwhite and hence ineligible for citizenship.

After 1910 most individuals from East Asia who applied for citizenship were refused. Burmese, Malaysian, Thai, Indian, and Korean applicants were flatly rejected by the courts as ineligible nonwhite aliens. Persons of mixed parentage could also be rejected: in 1912 a federal court turned down a "half-breed German and Japanese" and a federal court excluded a "quarter-breed Spaniard and Filipino."

Aliens from the Near East and Middle East were also subjected to close scrutiny and in several cases were denied citizenship. The 1910 U.S. Census classified Syrians, Armenians, Palestinians, Persians, and Turks as "Asiatics." These people had usually received citizenship papers, but after the directive of 1910 some of these applicants encountered difficulty in securing citizenship. A few had to resort to litigation to overturn the rulings of naturalization officers who wished to exclude them.

In the 1920s federal attorneys brought suit against a number of aliens suspected of having fraudulently acquired certificates of naturalization. In Michigan a U.S. court revoked the citizenship of an Arab from western India. The defendant claimed that his Arab ancestors had not intermarried with "the native stock of India" and "kept their Arabian blood line clear and pure," but the judge held that the Arab was disqualified on the grounds of race alone. In Oregon another revocation hearing involved a naturalized Armenian. Citing Strabo's *Geography*, Herodotus's *History*, and the testimony of a pair of well-known anthropologists, Franz Boas and Roland Dixon, this time the court found that the defendant was qualified for naturalization. It is now "judicially determined," the court remarked, "that the mere color of the skin of the individual does not afford a practical test as to whether he is eligible to American citizenship."

The Supreme Court was equally contradictory in its reasoning and criteria in determining eligibility for citizenship. In 1922 it decided that scientific tests had to be applied because misleading physical characteristics could be found "even among Anglo-Saxons," but the next year it held that a high-caste Hindu was ineligible for citizenship because, although in anthropological terms he was descended from the same stock as Europeans, he was not white by the definition of the common man.

States also used the category of "aliens ineligible for citizenship" to establish local laws restricting certain people from acquiring property and working in specified occupations. California, in particular, experimented with a variety of laws limiting the occupations that Chinese could hold, but all of them were swiftly struck down by federal courts as violating the "equal protection of the laws" guaranteed by the Fourteenth Amendment to alien and citizen alike. The phrase "equal protection of the laws," however, was then interpreted by the Court as requiring equal treatment only to those persons of a specified class. Legislation was not invalidated by the Fourteenth Amendment if it affected equally all persons placed by law in a special classification for a reasonable purpose. A state could enact laws that discriminated against all aliens or certain kinds of aliens—those who had not filed a declaration of intention or those who were ineligible for citizenship—as a class.

Several states used this qualification to erect laws prohibiting aliens ineligible for citizenship from acquiring or transferring property. A California law of 1913 raised that barrier against Asians. It was directed especially against the Japanese, who had acquired and developed sizable amounts of agricultural land by that time. The classification of aliens ineligible for citizenship was rationalized on the grounds that their allegiance was doubtful enough to warrant special treatment. In the 1930s, nine states, all but one of them (Florida) in the West, prohibited Asian aliens from purchasing real property.

Many states took the rule of equal treatment for a specified category of persons as a warrant to impose restrictions on all aliens. In the 1930s, 18 states imposed on them various restrictions on acquiring property; 15 placed limitations on both the amount of property and the length of time it could be held. Some states also limited alien employment through the exercise of their police power. States empowered to manage natural resources and public works used that authority to discriminate legally against alien employment in the civil service and public works, and severely restricted their purchase of fishing and hunting licenses. Most states excluded aliens from practicing law and medicine and some prohibited them from dentistry, pharmacy, engineering, and optometry (see Table 4.1). In 1890 the Maryland legislature restricted retail liquor licenses to citizens on the grounds that they would be more concerned about social conditions and less likely to permit abuses. A Cincinnati municipal ordinance denied aliens licenses to operate poolrooms. In 1927 an alien plaintiff who challenged this law brought his case before the Supreme Court, claiming that his Fourteenth Amendment rights had been violated. The Court, in finding against the plaintiff, held that poolrooms had a strong potential for antisocial activity and that citizen proprietors were less likely than alien ones to allow their establishments to become public nuisances.

Several of these laws were struck down by federal courts on Fourteeth Amendment principles. The most radical anti-

Table 4.1. Occupations prohibited to aliens, 1941.

Occupation	States requiring citizenship
Physician	28
Attorney	26[a]
Certified public accountant	15
Pharmacist	14
Dentist	11
Optometrist	11
Teacher	10
Mine inspector, foreman	10
Engineer and land surveyor	8
Bank director	7
Architect	6
Pilot of vessels	6
Barber	5
Master plumber	4
Registered nurse	4

Source: William S. Bernard, *American Immigration Policy* (New York, 1950), p. 116.

a. Some 26 of 48 states required by law that an attorney be a citizen; in 12 others, court ruling made citizenship mandatory for admission to the bar.

alien law, an Arizona statute requiring that 80 percent of all employees in every business employing more than five persons had to be citizens, was declared in violation of the Fourteenth Amendment in 1915 by the U.S. Supreme Court.

Laws restricting the economic activity of aliens proliferated in the early 20th century, through the authority of a state's police power and the principle of separate classification, but alien civil rights were still generally secured by the Fourteenth Amendment, which extended the due process of law and its equal protection to all "persons" whether or not they were citizens. The courts unanimously agreed that aliens were to receive protection under its terms.

A vestige of the common law of naturalization functioned

as a barrier to intermarriage between male aliens and female citizens in the early 20th century. After 1855 the United States followed the doctrine that an alien wife acquired the citizenship of her American husband. But then the converse of that principle—that any American woman who married an alien assumed the nationality of her husband—was established by a congressional act of 1907. Not only was the wife of an alien stripped of her citizenship, but she was not eligible for naturalization unless her husband was naturalized first, again on the principle that the nationality of the wife followed that of her husband.

This dependency was terminated by the Cable Act of 1922, which conferred independent citizenship on married women, after the passage of the Nineteenth Amendment granting women full political rights made the dependency of women's citizenship increasingly anomalous. Henceforth no female citizen could lose her U.S. citizenship by marriage to an alien, and no alien woman could acquire citizenship either by marriage to an American or by the naturalization of her husband. The Cable Act had been supported by those seeking to enfranchise women who had lost their citizenship through marriage, after the Nineteenth Amendment had given women the right to vote. The principle of independent citizenship would also provide protection against the political power of foreign women who had obtained citizenship, and thereby voting rights, simply by marrying U.S. citizens. Female citizens who married aliens ineligible for citizenship continued to be deprived of citizenship, however; that measure was not repealed until 1931. The laws of 1922 and 1931 on marriage and naturalization had two results. More male aliens could be assimilated through marriage to American women. The assimilation of foreign women was made to go hand in hand with the raising of standards for American citizenship; female aliens would no longer have an easy or automatic path to citizenship.

The expansion of the United States beyond its continental limits posed new problems for developing a workable concept of American nationality. The peoples inhabiting Alaska, Hawaii, the Philippines, Puerto Rico, and other territorial possessions had to be incorporated into the framework of an imperial order. Alaska, acquired by purchase in 1867, and Hawaii, annexed in 1898, became "incorporated territories" by congressional act, which meant that they were subject to the Constitution and that their inhabitants were citizens of the United States. Members of indigenous tribes were considered wards of the U.S. government.

The political and civil status of the inhabitants of the Philippines and Puerto Rico, also acquired by cession in 1898, raised more complicated problems. In the Insular Cases of 1901–1903 the Supreme Court determined that the Philippines and Puerto Rico were not incorporated by the United States, but were "appurtenant thereto as a possession"; their inhabitants were neither aliens nor citizens. For them the designation "national" was created; a national owed allegiance to the U.S. government, was permitted to enter and leave the United States at will, and was entitled to the protection of federal laws. In 1900 Congress made Puerto Rican inhabitants "citizens of Puerto Rico," and in 1902 it made Philippine inhabitants "citizens of the Philippine Islands." In 1917 it conferred American citizenship on those persons made citizens of Puerto Rico by the act of 1900, but inhabitants of other incorporated territories received different treatment. The people of the Virgin Islands were granted U.S. citizenship in 1927, but Congress chose not to define the civil status of the people of Guam, Samoa, and the Panama Canal Zone, simply considering them to be "inhabitants . . . entitled to the protection of the United States."

Racist beliefs and doubts about the assimilability of territorial peoples were again crucial factors in determining the policy that lay behind the creation of the category of national; the category placed these people in an inferior civil position and, at least in the case of Polynesian and most Filipino applicants, denied them the opportunity to become citizens through naturalization, on the grounds that they were racially ineligible for citizenship. William Howard Taft, while still civil governor of the Philippines, explained that the reason for this policy was that "tropical peoples cannot lift themselves as the Anglo-Saxons"; he firmly believed that the Filipinos were not capable of quick adaptation to self-government, an argument he used to justify the denial of independence to the islands. American citizenship was viewed as a delicate, precious handiwork; people unaccustomed to the practice and philosophy of democracy needed a long period of tutelage before they could develop the capacity to exercise its rights.

The position of the American Indians was affected by these views on the incorporation of territorial peoples. Throughout the 19th century, Indian tribes continued to be regarded as separate nations existing within the territory of the United States; as such, they were dealt with through treaties and acts of Congress. Congress had naturalized some Indians on an irregular basis through these treaties and other acts, and the Dawes Act of 1887 granted citizenship to Indians who had left the tribe for civil society; but not until 1924 did Congress grant citizenship to all Indians born within the jurisdiction of the U.S. government. At the same time their status was changed from one based on the separate-nation principle to one resembling that of inhabitants of the incorporated territories.

The Americanization Movement

Before World War I social reformers, legislators, and policy makers learned that the number of naturalized male adults had increased by only 7 percent from 1900 to 1910, while the number of alien adult males had increased by 73 percent. The proportion of aliens among all foreign-born adult males grew from 43 percent in 1900 to 55 percent in 1919 (see Table 4.2). Many policy makers feared that new immigrants from southern and eastern Europe were not making a serious effort to acquire U.S. citizenship. The U.S. Immigration Com-

Table 4.2. Aliens in the United States, 1890–1970.

Year	Total U.S. population	Number of aliens[a]	Aliens as percent of total population
1890	62,947,714	—	—
1900	75,994,575	—	—
1910	91,972,266	—	—
1920	105,710,620	7,430,809	7
1930	122,775,046	6,284,613	5
1940	131,669,275	4,314,631	3
1950	150,216,110	2,784,425	2
1960	179,325,657	—	—
1970	203,193,774		2

Year	Total foreign-born adult males	Adult male aliens[a]	Male aliens as percent of foreign-born adult males
1890	4,348,459	1,802,706	42
1900	5,010,286	2,161,479	43
1910	6,780,214	3,741,911	55
1920	7,063,594	3,743,368	53
1930	7,218,977	2,971,273	41
1940	5,969,588	1,893,381	32
1950	5,092,230	1,110,335	22
1960	4,382,844	—	—
1970	3,864,834	1,145,451	30

mission asserted in 1911 that there were critical differences between the old immigrants of northern and western Europe and the new eastern and southern European immigrants. The earlier immigrants had come to secure religious and political freedom and to help build a republican society, whereas the new immigrants had come only for material betterment. The recent arrivals had by and large come from countries whose government and religion were authoritarian, often even despotic; they had had no experience with

Table 4.2. (*Continued*)

Year	Total foreign-born adult females	Adult female aliens[a]	Female aliens as percent of foreign-born adult females
1890	—	—	—
1900	—	—	—
1910	—	—	—
1920	5,022,799	2,724,224	54
1930	6,117,376	2,683,399	44
1940	5,323,233	2,239,797	45
1950	4,928,220	1,443,670	29
1960	4,596,680	—	—
1970	4,655,564	1,579,920	34

Source: U.S. Bureau of the Census, *Historical Statistics of the United States, Colonial Times to 1970* (Washington, D.C., 1975), p. 116.

a. Includes those aliens who had filed a declaration of intention of citizenship, and those whose nationality was not reported. The Census Bureau indicated "that much the larger proportion of those for whom no report as to citizenship was secured were aliens."

democratic institutions or republican government; they had little intention of becoming citizens, and, even if they had, they were ill prepared to exercise democratic rights.

Partly in response to such concerns, Congress centralized and upgraded the naturalization procedure by forming a separate Bureau of Naturalization under the authority of a Commissioner of Naturalization in 1913. The bureau received all declarations, petitions, and naturalization approvals filed in the country; it administered the naturalization law, checked to see that only qualified applicants received citizenship, and served as a clearing-house for organized efforts to promote naturalization. The secretary of labor reported two years later that the naturalization examiners were withholding citizenship from large numbers of applicants ignorant of the American form of government, and this soon led to the organization of citizenship classes to teach petitioners for naturalization what they needed to know. The secretary estimated that 75 percent of all aliens could be transformed through citizenship classes into desirable citizenship material, and he recommended a national program to improve the quality of applicants.

In its first stages, bureau agents held conferences with public-school authorities in Chicago, St. Louis, Milwaukee, St. Paul, Minneapolis, Philadelphia, and New York in 1914 and in several other cities the next year. The delegates approved the idea of a cooperative movement between local public schools and the Bureau of Naturalization.

The bureau then conducted a national survey in 1915 to determine what efforts the public schools were making to prepare foreigners for citizenship, the nature of the citizenship courses they were offering, and the number attending their courses who were candidates for naturalization. The results showed that nearly all school systems in the larger cities offered citizenship classes for adults. New York City had the most extensive program: 1,000 classes in which 40,000 adult foreigners were enrolled. The classes taught English, basic writing, American history, and civics; attendance was often better than in the regular night-school courses. One school official saw a decided interest in the work and a determined desire to learn the English language and American customs and laws.

To aid the public schools, the Bureau of Naturalization sent the names and addresses of those who had filed first and second papers to school systems throughout the country and compiled and distributed a standardized textbook called *An Outline Course in Citizenship* (it was followed by other editions). The bureau also approached candidates for citizenship through letters exhorting them to attend citizenship courses, and it devised a "certificate of graduation," bearing signatures of bureau officials and local school authorities, which was presented to candidates when they became citizens.

Between 1913 and 1930 the Bureau of Naturalization coordinated its work with the efforts of the U.S. Bureau of Education and of citizens' organizations such as the National Americanization Committee, in order to promote and publicize the cause of naturalization. Progressive political reforms, such as the initiative and referendum, made it seem even more imperative that the foreign-born be educated in the duties of American citizenship and properly qualified for naturalization, especially those millions of newcomers from southern and eastern Europe whose notions of democracy were allegedly so underdeveloped.

Although these agencies showered immigrants with publicity and propaganda, they were aware that naturalization should not be coerced. They wanted to have as citizens only those who wanted to be citizens, who had sufficient interest in American society and politics to participate in civic life, and who possessed sufficient intelligence to make sensible political decisions. The principle underlying the movement was that the active participatory citizenship they projected as the goal of assimilation could only be secured if the naturalization process that led up to it was voluntary and popular. To compel foreigners to naturalize would be self-defeating; the indifferent, the reluctant, and the disloyal should not be encouraged. Spectacular Fourth of July celebrations, patriotic parades, and mass naturalization ceremonies were held in the major immigrant population centers to dramatize the significance of U.S. citizenship and to directly involve masses of foreigners as participants in civic culture.

During the twenties and thirties social scientists began to study the naturalization rates of alien groups in an attempt to gauge how this Americanization campaign was progressing. Statistical studies of naturalization cases showed that the foreign-born with the longest residence were also the most likely to have been naturalized, and that, generally speaking, immigrants took considerably longer than the minimum five years to acquire citizenship. New immigrant groups took an average of 10.6 years, a figure that policy makers liked to interpret as confirming their theory that those people had a low degree of civic consciousness, although attempts were also made to refute that notion by showing that naturalization rates correlated better with education, occupation, and income than with ethnic background. On the other hand, whatever the reasons, one study showed that some new immigrant groups were taking an average of 20 years to acquire citizenship, although a host of government and private studies revealed that many were making an enormous effort to become naturalized.

The civic organizations of various nationality groups organized courses in English-language instruction and American history for applicants. In New Jersey in 1920 the Passaic Local of the Amalgamated Textile Workers of America, the union with the largest membership of aliens in the state, started classes in English and citizenship and planned to add courses in history, economics, and government. It was often very difficult for the immigrants to attend them, however. State bureaus of education conducted interviews that revealed over and over the serious obstacles these mostly poor and working-class people had to overcome in order to get to classes. They worked at night when the classes were held, or had to mind the children while the wife went to work, or were simply too exhausted after a hard day's factory labor. Nevertheless many managed it. The Massachusetts Department of Education reported the sacrifices involved as "both inspiring and pathetic." A Plymouth man rode ten miles after work, often without his supper, to attend his class; in Shirley, a group of Polish men went to class three nights a week, and their wives attended the other two while they looked after the children; a French Canadian resident of

Melrose worked nights, and cut short his sleep to attend classes during the day. Although the average course lasted seven months and classes were held nearly every day, Cambridge reported 220 students with a 100-percent-attendance record for the whole term. In Worcester over 89 percent of those enrolled at the beginning of the term were still there at the end, and students in other towns had similar records.

These reports reflect the growing conviction on the part of many resident aliens that U.S. citizenship would give them the rights, privileges, and protections guaranteed by the federal government; they would live, vote, and secure work on the same basis as native U.S. citizens and would escape the restrictions and encumbrances of alien status. Citizenship also meant acceptance as an American: it was an unimpeachable sign that the newcomer had assimilated and had become equal as a result of possessing a set of rights that he or she had not known as an alien.

Along with this Americanization campaign, World War I had brought with it a wartime patriotism that combined nationalism, xenophobia, and constant fears about alien "subversion." In 1917 a federal law mandated deportation for any alien who at any time after his entry into the United States had advocated revolution or sabotage, and in the following year over 7,000 enemy aliens were arrested by the Justice Department, many of them German Americans; some were interned. To avoid any possibility that alien voters might gain control of local elections, in 1918 three states abolished alien suffrage.

After the war, frequent strikes and bombings by radicals aggravated the wartime mood. Using the 1917 deportation law as the basis for summary arrests and persecutions, Attorney General A. Mitchell Palmer jailed 6,000 suspects in 1920, including many citizens and many who were neither radicals, nor socialists, nor Communists; 600 aliens were actually deported. Although the attorney general repeatedly asked Congress for a general sedition law, he did not get one, and Secretary of Labor William B. Wilson at least saw to it that the deportation hearings were conducted according to the rules of evidence and fair play.

After World War I naturalization was denied by the courts to men who had been conscientious objectors, or who confessed conscientious scruples against the shedding of blood, or who lacked a clear attachment "to the principles of the Constitution." The U.S. Supreme Court denied citizenship to pacifists. Socialists, Communists, and other radicals were called into court by U.S. attorneys and their citizenship papers canceled. The Supreme Court in 1920 revoked the papers of a German American who had defended the sinking of the *Lusitania* and had "praised the attitude of Germany" during the war. Although he had filed his first papers in 1904, the Court ruled that his subsequent activities demonstrated that he had not made the declaration in "full faith," and his papers were confiscated. Throughout the 1920s courts went to extreme lengths and used questionable criteria to test for loyalty to the United States when they reviewed naturalization cases.

National Security and Liberalizing Naturalization, 1941 to the Present

Notions about alien subversives persisted into the thirties, and the thousands of central European refugees fleeing fascism often received a rather cautious welcome. The strict security screening they underwent sent over 117,000 aliens back to where they had come from, many disqualified on political grounds (see Table 4.3). As the European situation became more tense the federal government took additional steps to protect national security and to monitor the activities of aliens. Congress passed the Alien Registration Act of 1940, which required the fingerprinting and registering of over 5 million aliens in the country. When the United States entered the war at the end of 1941, over 1 million people were classified as "enemy aliens" and had a variety of restrictions placed upon their activities; eventually they were

Table 4.3. Aliens deported, 1892–1970.

Years	Number
1892–1900	3,127
1901–1910	11,558
1911–1920	27,912
1921–1930	92,157
1931–1940	117,086
1941–1950	110,849
1951–1960	129,887
1961–1970	96,374

Source: U.S. Bureau of the Census, *Historical Statistics of the United States, Colonial Times to 1970* (Washington, D.C., 1975), p. 114.

reclassified as "aliens of enemy nationality," and many of these restrictions were abolished. Over 600,000 Italians were placed in this category, along with 35,000 Japanese and thousands of Germans. No further steps were taken against most Germans and Italians, but all persons of Japanese origin or ancestry, alien and citizen alike, living on the West Coast were detained in relocation camps from 1942 to 1945.

The drive for national security and wartime victory produced several changes in the naturalization law. A reorganized and combined Immigration and Naturalization Service was transferred in 1940 from the Department of Labor to the Justice Department. Under the jurisdiction of the attorney general, the service was able to coordinate its activities with those of Justice Department agents in charge of national security. Congress enacted the Nationality Act of 1940 which unified and tightened the scattered and confusing naturalization statutes enacted since 1906. The act still barred Filipinos and other Asian nationals from becoming citizens, but it opened up naturalization to indigenous territorial peoples such as the Aleuts and Eskimos. The ban on the immigration and naturalization of the Chinese was lifted in 1943 as a gesture of good will toward America's Chinese allies, and in

1946 the ban on citizenship was lifted against Filipinos and East Indians in a similar gesture of acknowledgment of their resistance to the common enemy.

After World War II the Cold War became a primary force shaping the development of federal policy toward aliens. Internal subversion and the threat of war against the Communist powers absorbed the attention of Congress, which responded with two major bills—the Internal Security Act of 1950 and the McCarran-Walter Immigration and Nationality Act of 1952. The 1950 act revived the 1940 Alien Registration Act, and required that all aliens register and report their current address to the Immigration and Naturalization Service in January of each year. It also stipulated that anyone who had ever been a Communist party member could be excluded from entry or deported.

The McCarran-Walter Act of 1952 recodified and updated the myriad immigration and naturalization statutes that had been passed in the previous half-century. This gigantic 300-page omnibus bill relaxed the restrictions on alleged ex-Communists, but enormously strengthened the federal government's deportation powers and widened its surveillance of alien residents. Aliens who became affiliated with any group or effort to oppose the U.S. government, who advocated or taught the destruction of property, who became drug addicts, or who were connected with immoral practices or an "immoral place" could be deported at any time after entry. The law gave federal officials blanket authority for prosecuting deportation cases. In the 1950s over 130,000 aliens were deported, the highest number of deportations ever ordered in a ten-year period. Many of them, however, did not come under these provisions, but were simply illegal Mexican itinerant workers. Some were the same individuals deported repeatedly.

The McCarran-Walter Act also established a new requirement that significantly raised the qualifications for citizenship: an applicant not only had to be able to speak and understand English, but he had to be able to read and write "simple words and phrases." Despite this raising of qualifications, the number of rejected petitioners was 66 percent lower in the 1950s than it had been the decade before.

The most important change in naturalization policy, however, was the abolition of all racial tests or marital qualifications for citizenship. The act declared that "the right of a person to become a naturalized citizen of the United States shall not be denied or abridged because of race or sex or because such person is married." Thus all persons were permitted for the first time by a general federal law to apply individually for naturalization and to be considered purely on the bases of merit and qualification. At one stroke the arbitrary category of "aliens ineligible for citizenship," which had consigned Asian nationalities to the inferior status of permanent-resident aliens for nearly a century, was swept away. The procedures and requirements for naturalization as a U.S. citizen remain today essentially the same as those set forth in the McCarran-Walter Act.

The composition of the foreign-born population seeking naturalization changed gradually in the next three decades. From 1900 to 1940, the vast majority of naturalized persons came from countries in Europe. In the 1970s, by contrast, a large number of naturalized citizens have come from elsewhere: some of the leading providers of naturalized immigrants have been China, Taiwan, Korea, Mexico, the Philippines, Canada, and the West Indies.

Throughout the 20th century, time of arrival and rate of return migration have been strongly correlated with naturalization patterns. In the early decades of the century, immigrants from northern and western European nations, who had resided longest in the United States, had the highest proportions of naturalized persons, while immigrants from southern and eastern European countries, more recent arrivals, had the lowest percentages of naturalized persons (see Table 4.4). Sixty-three percent of the English foreign-born, 69 percent of the Swedish foreign-born, and 72 percent of the German foreign-born were U.S. citizens in 1920; how-

Table 4.4. Percentage of foreign-born persons naturalized, by country of origin, 1910–1970.[a]

Country	1910[b]	1920[c]	1930[c]	1950[c]	1970
All countries	45.6	48.7	58.8	67.9	63.6
England	59.4	63.1	67.0 }	74.8 }	65.3
Wales	69.2	72.9	73.8 }		
Scotland	56.5	60.9	53.5	— }	
Northern Ireland	— }	65.7	68.1	—	—
Ireland	67.8 }		66.1	79.7	81.8
Norway	57.1	67.3	70.9	82.4	82.5
Sweden	62.8	69.0	72.6	84.5	85.3
Denmark	61.6 }	69.2	74.9	—	82.2
Iceland	— }		68.3	—	—
Netherlands	56.8	56.0	66.6	—	69.5
Belgium	} 43.0	49.0	65.2	—	—
Luxembourg	}	72.5	80.3	—	—
Switzerland	61.8	64.9	67.4	—	70.5
France	49.6	56.7	63.1	—	65.5
Germany	69.5	72.8	70.5	80.1	77.5[d]
Poland	—	28.0	50.5	72.0	80.2
Czechoslovakia	—	45.8	61.3	77.5	85.0
Austria	24.6	37.7	63.0	79.5	86.9
Hungary	14.3	29.1	55.7	—	83.4
Yugoslavia	—	25.1	46.3	—	71.0
Russia	26.1 }		62.2	82.7[e]	88.5
Latvia	— }	40.2	60.9	—	—
Estonia	— }		42.3	—	—
Lithuania	—	25.6	47.5	—	80.1
Finland	30.6	41.3	51.0	—	75.1
Romania	28.8	41.1	60.3	—	81.3
Bulgaria	—	12.1	38.3	—	—
Turkey in Europe	—	20.2	45.1	—	—
Greece	—	16.8	44.7	—	65.2
Albania	—	7.4	31.7	—	—
Italy	17.7	28.1	50.0	79.5	79.2
Spain	16.4	9.9	18.9	—	—
Portugal	24.9	16.4	18.7	—	—
Other Europe	35.6	48.0	47.8	—	61.0
Armenia	—	28.9	46.8	—	—
Palestine	—	37.5	56.5	—	—
Syria	—	28.9	50.9	—	—

Table 4.4. (*Continued*)

Country	1910[b]	1920[c]	1930[c]	1950[c]	1970
Turkey in Asia	21.2	25.1	46.0	—	—
Other Asia	33.4	36.5	41.9	—	38.5
Canada, French	44.7	44.8	46.9	72.3 ⎱	63.4
Canada, Other ⎱	53.9	57.9	53.4	71.0 ⎰	
Newfoundland ⎰		47.4	38.8	—	—
Cuba ⎱	30.6	21.1	22.2	—	24.3
Other West Indies ⎰		34.8	45.8	—	—
Mexico	10.7	5.9	23.8	26.3	38.8
Central and South America	34.8	24.1	28.8	—	—
Africa ⎤		43.6	51.1	—	—
Australia		49.5	59.3	—	—
Azores		20.7	24.4	—	—
Other Atlantic islands ⎬	32.3	22.2	34.7	—	—
Pacific islands		50.1	54.2	—	—
Not specified		37.4	32.4	—	—
Born at sea ⎦		54.4	57.7	—	—

Source: U.S. Bureau of the Census, *13th Census of the United States, 1910* (Washington, D.C., 1913), I, *Population,* p. 1068; U.S. Bureau of the Census, *15th Census of the United States, 1930* (Washington, D.C., 1933), II, *Population,* pp. 406–407; U.S. Bureau of the Census, *Census of the Population, 1950* (Washington, D.C., 1954), *Special Reports,* pt. 3, ch. A, p. 130; U.S. Bureau of the Census, *Census of the Population, 1970,* I, *Characteristics of the Population* (Washington, D.C., 1973), pt. 1, p. 600.

  a. Data for 1940 and 1960 not available.
  b. Percentage of foreign-born white persons 21 years and older.
  c. Includes only foreign-born white persons.
  d. Includes East and West Germany
  e. Excludes persons of Ukrainian origin.

ever, only 7 percent of the Albanian, 12 percent of the Bulgarian, 17 percent of the Greek, 28 percent of the Polish and Italian, and 29 percent of the Hungarian foreign-born were naturalized. The foreign-born from southern and eastern Europe were also those who returned in very large proportions to their home countries. When the flow of immigrants decreased after 1924, the proportion of the naturalized foreign-born from southern and eastern Europe climbed until it equaled or exceeded the proportion of naturalized newcomers from northern and western Europe. By 1950, for example, nearly 80 percent of foreign-born Italians had secured citizenship, as compared with 75 percent of immigrants from the United Kingdom. Time of arrival and rate of return migration have also been related to the naturalization of immigrants arriving in the last two decades from Mexico, the West Indies, Central and South America, and East Asian countries. These recently arrived peoples returned home often; as a consequence, they have had low naturalization percentages.

In 1940 more than half the total alien population resided in the Northeast and Midwest, mainly in New York, New Jersey, Pennsylvania, Massachusetts, Michigan, and Illinois. Since that time the concentration of alien population has shifted westward with the overall distribution of the nation's population. Signifying this trend, the 1970 Census reported that California had replaced New York as the state with the largest number of resident aliens.

The highest percentage of aliens in the population was recorded in the 1920 U.S. Census and has been declining gradually ever since. In 1920, 7 percent of the population was alien; in 1940, 3 percent. In 1950 the alien population was only 2 percent of the country's population, and remained at that level up to 1970. It is important to bear in mind that these statistics refer only to those aliens enumerated in the decennial census, which do not record accurately aliens residing illegally in the country.

From 1900 the average number of aliens annually naturalized steadily increased and peaked at World War II, as a result of the large number of aliens acquiring citizenship through military service (see Table 4.5). The drop in the alien population after the war led to a decline in annual naturalizations. In the 1950s the number of naturalizations was 50 percent of the total from 1940 to 1950. On the annual average, more alien women than men have been naturalized each year since 1940, chiefly because the population of adult female aliens has been greater than that of male aliens since that time.

The alien population has become significantly younger since World War II. In 1944, 72 percent of the alien population was under 60 years of age; in 1970, 88 percent was under 65, and 70 percent was under 44.

The growth in the alien population spurred by the liberal Hart-Celler Immigration Act of 1965 has produced a steady rise in the number of naturalizations each year. In 1975, for example, about 142,000 persons were naturalized, 8 percent

Table 4.5. Alien naturalization, 1907–1976.

Period	Average number of petitions for naturalization per year		Average number of naturalization certificates issued per year	
	Filed	Denied	Male	Female
1907–1910	41,000	4,425	—	—
1911–1920	138,140	11,870	—	—
1921–1930	188,430	16,550	116,620	25,520
1931–1940	163,710	4,580	96,840	55,010
1941–1950	193,810	6,480	94,150	104,550
1951–1960	123,050	2,760	50,350	68,640
1961–1970	114,300	2,360	51,350	60,680
1971–1976	140,566	2,466	63,166	71,700

Source: U.S. Department of Commerce, *Statistical Abstract of the United States, 1977* (Washington, D.C., 1977), p. 89.

more than the approximately 132,000 naturalized the year before.

The alien population today is younger than that of 1940; ethnic groups from the Western Hemisphere and Asia are more heavily represented, and aliens are geographically more evenly distributed between the Atlantic and Pacific coasts. Recently policy makers have been concerned with the presence of a large population of illegal aliens who have migrated from Mexico across land borders to settle and work in the Southwest. Some steps have been taken to restrict their entry, to deport them, and to penalize their employers, but a systematic policy toward these aliens remains unformulated.

The development of American citizenship has been a vital ingredient in the forming of an American nation out of a multiplicity of ethnic groups. The history of citizenship has revealed the changing relationship of the individual citizen to the political structure of the nation. Citizenship was created in the American Revolution as each inhabitant placed his consent in republican government, by that voluntary act approving its sovereignty and binding his allegiance to it.

The political structure of the republic was neither securely integrated nor clearly defined in law in the first half of the 19th century. Sectional conflict between slave states and free states was mirrored in an ambiguous constitutional idea of citizenship in which competing allegiances to state and federal governments clashed.

The Civil War and Reconstruction brought a new and enduring unity to the national polity and established the primacy of the federal government. As Reconstruction amendments were passed to extend constitutional protection and national citizenship to blacks as well as whites, the status of U.S. citizenship became decisively national in scope and federal in origin. The states, however, were still accorded through Supreme Court decisions primary control over the personal, property, and civil rights of their inhabitants; the sphere of the immunities and privileges of federal citizenship were to be strictly limited to the general protections articulated in the Constitution and federal statutes.

In the late 19th and early 20th centuries the presence of aliens arriving through immigration and as a result of territorial acquisition forced open the boundaries of American nationality. A hierarchy of civil ranks—aliens ineligible for citizenship, territorial nationals, declarants for citizenship—proliferated to control the incorporation of new immigrant groups and to threaten the traditional concept of a unitary American citizenship. Naturalization had been a casual and informal process, but gradually crude racist criteria and upgraded naturalization standards were applied to admit only "suitable" aliens. The process of including new peoples was tempered by favoritism toward those thought to be more racially compatible and better prepared for civic duties. The unfamiliarity of some new immigrants with democratic government, their acquaintance with monarchical regimes and authoritarian religions, and their ignorance of English cast doubt in the minds of nativists as to their readiness for citizenship rights.

The trend toward restriction was counterbalanced by a powerful drive toward assimilation. While certain racial groups were excluded from naturalization, the vast majority of aliens continued to be accepted for citizenship. They were exposed to a widespread campaign led by government and private organizations to promote the speedy acquisition of American citizenship, especially during the Americanization drive of the World War I era. Schools became the vehicles for the civic education of immigrants and their children which would prepare them for the responsibilities and duties of citizenship. The movement for citizenship encouraged voluntary, popular naturalization.

By the mid-20th century the racial restrictions on naturalization seemed both impolitic and impractical. Experience had shown that all ethnic groups, given time and encouragement, had the capacity to assimilate into the national civic culture, and so U.S. citizenship was opened to all.

Broader access to citizenship and expanded federal safeguards over the rights of citizens accompanied the building of a more centralized government. As the powers of the federal government grew and its jurisdiction was gradually extended to encompass more aspects of social life, every person had to be placed in a single and consistent relation to the federal authority through citizenship. Fears that ethnocultural or racial background could inhibit the proper exercise of citizenship rights were supplanted by a confidence that citizenship was a transcendent status obtainable by all individuals who shared a common membership in a democratic polity.

BIBLIOGRAPHY

1. Economic and Social Characteristics of the Immigrants

No single work covers the topic. Works with fairly general coverage include, by demographers, Warren S. Thompson and P.K. Whelpton, *Population Trends in the United States* (1933; reprint, New York, 1969), and Conrad Taeuber and Irene Taeuber, *The Changing Population of the United States* (New York, 1958), and, by historians, Marcus Lee Hansen, *The Atlantic Migration, 1607–1860* (Cambridge, Mass., 1940), and Oscar Handlin, ed., *Immigration as a Factor in American History* (Englewood Cliffs, N.J., 1959). More specific studies, focusing chiefly on the period from 1790 to 1950, or parts thereof, include Simon Kuznets and Ernest Rubin, *Immigration and the Foreign Born* (New York, 1954), on net versus gross immigration flows; Niles Carpenter, *Immigrants and Their Children, 1920* (Washington, 1927), on national origins; Stanley Lebergott, *Manpower in Economic Growth: The American Record Since 1800* (New York, 1964), and Edward P. Hutchinson, *Immigrants and Their Children, 1850–1950* (New York, 1956), on labor force and occupations; and Simon Kuznets et al., *Population Redistribution and Economic Growth, United States, 1870–1950,* 3 vols. (Philadelphia, 1957–1964), covering internal migration of the foreign born. Fluctuations in immigration are analyzed by Harry Jerome, *Migration and Business Cycles* (New York, 1926); Richard A. Easterlin, *Population, Labor Force, and Long Swings in Economic Growth: The American Experience* (New York, 1968); and Brinley Thomas, *Migration and Economic Growth,* 2d ed. (Cambridge, England, 1973). Brinley Thomas, ed., *Economics of International Migration* (London, 1958), focuses on economic causes and effects of migration. Two studies relating to the colonial period are J. Potter, "The Growth of Population in America, 1700–1860," in *Population in History,* eds. C.V. Glass and D.E.C. Eversley (Chicago, 1965); and P.M.G. Harris, "The Social Origins of American Leaders: The Demographic Foundations," *Perspectives in American History* 3 (1969): 159–344. Edward P. Hutchinson, ed., "The New Immigration," *The Annals of the American Academy of Political and Social Sciences* 367 (September 1966): 1–149, and Charles B. Keely, "Immigration Composition and Population Policy," in *Population: Dynamics, Ethics and Policy,* eds. Priscilla Reining and Irene Tinker (Washington, D.C., 1975), discuss recent immigration. The best works on immigration policy are Marion T. Bennett, *American Immigration Policies* (Washington, D.C., 1963), and Robert A. Divine, *American Immigration Policy, 1924–1952* (1957; reprint, New York, 1972). Major data sources are the U.S. Bureau of the Census, *Historical Statistics of the United States, Colonial Times to 1970* (Washington, D.C., 1975); U.S. Immigration and Naturalization Service, *Annual Reports* (Washington, D.C., 1819–); U.S. Senate, 61st Congress, 3rd Session, Doc. No. 747, Reports of the Immigration Commission, *Abstracts of Reports of the Immigration Commission* (Washington, D.C., 1911); and Walter F. Willcox, ed., *International Migrations* (New York, 1929).

2.   Settlement Patterns and Spatial Distribution

The two most comprehensive overviews of the regional patterns of ethnic groups are Wilbur Zelinsky, *The Cultural Geography of the United States* (Englewood Cliffs, N.J., 1973), and Raymond D. Gastil, *Cultural Regions of the United States* (Seattle, 1975). Of several studies of individual ethnic groups, those by Donald W. Meinig, "The Mormon Culture Region: Strategies and Patterns in the Geography of the American West, 1847–1964," *Annals of the Association of American Geographers* 55 (1965): 191–220, and by Terry G. Jordan, "The Imprint of the Upper and Lower South on Mid-Nineteenth-Century Texas," *Annals of the A.A.G.* 57 (1967): 667–690, are exemplary. A fine collection of articles on the urban residential patterns of ethnic groups, including the study by Nathan Kantrovitz of segregation in the New York–New Jersey metropolitan area, have been edited by Ceri Peach, *Urban Social Segregation* (New York, 1975). Many of the controversial aspects of urban ethnicity are discussed in Nathan Glazer and Daniel P. Moynihan,

Beyond the Melting Pot, rev. ed. (Cambridge, Mass., 1972), while a comparative review of several cities is found in Stanley Lieberson, *Ethnic Patterns in American Cities* (Glencoe, Ill., 1963). A useful overview of the changing composition and circumstances of immigration is Leonard Dinnerstein and David M. Reimers, *Ethnic Americans: A History of Immigration and Assimilation* (New York, 1975). A more specifically geographic treatment of immigrant destinations is found in David Ward, *Cities and Immigrants: A Geography of Change in Nineteenth-Century America* (New York, 1971). For the colonial period, see James T. Lemon, *The Best Poor Man's Country* (Baltimore, 1972), a regional case study of the geography of ethnic pluralism in southeastern Pennsylvania. The changing distributions of blacks, Asians, American Indians, and Spanish-speaking groups are treated in Donald K. Fellows, *A Mosaic of America's Ethnic Minorities* (New York, 1972). Among the many case studies of the residential patterns of individual ethnic groups in specific cities, a recent classic is Kathleen N. Conzen, *Immigrant Milwaukee 1836–1860: Accommodation and Community in a Frontier City* (Cambridge, Mass., 1976). Other case studies are Paul A. Groves and Edward K. Muller, "The Evolution of Black Residential Areas in Late 19th-century Cities," *Journal of Historical Geography* 1 (1975): 169–191, and Caroline Golab, *Immigrant Destinations* (Philadelphia, 1977). Examinations of the residential patterns of southern cities in the 19th century are extremely rare; an exception is John P. Radford, "Race, Residence and Ideology: Charleston, South Carolina in the Mid-Nineteenth Century," *Journal of Historical Geography* 2 (1976): 329–346.

3. A History of U.S. Immigration Policy

General works on the history of American immigration are Edith Abbott, ed., *Historical Aspects of the Immigration Problem* (1926; reprint, New York, 1969); Maurice R. Davie, *World Immigration, with Special Reference to the United States* (New York, 1936); Leonard Dinnerstein and David Reimers, *Ethnic Americans: A History of Immigration and Assimilation* (New York, 1975); Oscar Handlin, ed., *Immigration as a Factor in American History* (Englewood Cliffs, N.J., 1959), and *The Uprooted*, 2d ed. (Boston, 1973); Marcus Lee Hansen, *The Atlantic Migration, 1607–1860* (1940; reprint, Cambridge,

1951); Maldwyn Jones, *American Immigration* (1960; reprint, Chicago, 1967); Philip Taylor, *The Distant Magnet* (London, 1971). Interpretive studies of immigration policy are Marion T. Bennet, *American Immigration Policies* (Washington, D.C., 1963); William S. Bernard, ed., *American Immigration Policy: A Reappraisal* (New York, 1950); idem, "American Immigration Policy: Its Evolution and Sociology," *International Migration* 3:4 (Geneva, 1965); Robert A. Divine, *American Immigration Policy, 1924–1952* (1957; reprint, New York, 1972); Roy Garis, *Immigration Restriction* (New York, 1928); Charles Price, *The Great White Walls are Built* (Canberra, 1974); Emberson E. Proper, *Colonial Immigration Laws* (New York, 1900).

Informative discussions of the social and intellectual factors shaping American immigration policy are found in Ray A. Billington, *The Protestant Crusade, 1800–1860: A Study of the Origins of American Nativism* (1938; reprint, Chicago, 1964); Oscar Handlin, *Race and Nationality in American Life* (Boston, 1957); John Higham, *Strangers in the Land* (New York, 1963) and *Send These to Me* (New York, 1975); Barbara M. Solomon, *Ancestors and Immigrants* (1956; reprint, Chicago, 1972).

4.   Naturalization and Citizenship

Informative legal studies on citizenship and naturalization in the United States are Frank G. Franklin, *The Legislative History of Naturalization in the United States From the Revolutionary War to 1861* (1906; reprint, New York, 1969); Luella Gettys, *The Law of Citizenship in the United States* (Chicago, 1934); John P. Roche, *The Early Development of United States Citizenship* (Ithaca, N.Y., 1949); I-Mien Tsiang, *The Question of Expatriation in America Prior to 1907* (Baltimore, 1942); Frederick Van Dyne, *A Treatise on the Law of Naturalization of the United States* (Washington, D.C., 1907); and John S. Wise, *A Treatise on American Citizenship* (Northport, N.Y., 1906). An important historical study of citizenship is James H. Kettner, *The Development of American Citizenship, 1607–1870* (Chapel Hill, N.C., 1978). Morton Keller, *Affairs of State* (Cambridge, Mass., 1977), provides an account of the impact of late-19th-century immigration and territorial acquisition on citizenship and naturalization. Also illuminating is Oscar and Mary Handlin, *The Dimensions of Liberty* (Cambridge, Mass., 1961).

The most helpful works on the status and rights of aliens are Norman Alexander, *Rights of Aliens under the Federal Constitution* (Montpelier, Vt., 1931); Max J. Kohler "Un-American Character of Race Legislation," *Annals of the American Academy* 34 (1909): 275–293; Milton R. Konvitz, *The Alien and the Asiatic in American Law* (1946; reprint, Ithaca, N.Y., 1965); and Norman MacKenzie, *The Legal Status of Aliens in Pacific Countries* (London, 1937). Racial restrictions in the naturalization law are discussed in D.O. McGovney, "American Citizenship," *Columbia Law Review* 11 (1911): 231–250, 326–347; and "Race Discrimination in Naturalization," *Iowa Law Bulletin* 8 (1923): 129–161, 211–244.

The social process of naturalization in the early 20th century is studied by William S. Bernard, "Cultural Determinants of Naturalization," *American Sociological Review* 1 (1936): 943–953; Niles Carpenter, *Immigrants and Their Children, 1920* (Washington, D.C., 1927); and John P. Gavit, *Americans by Choice* (1922; reprint, Montclair, N.J., 1971).

The most useful histories of the Americanization movement are Edward G. Hartmann, *The Movement to Americanize the Immigrant* (1948; reprint, New York, 1967); John Higham, *Strangers in the Land* (New York, 1963); and Gerd Korman, *Industrialization, Immigrants, and Americanizers* (Madison, Wis., 1967). Interesting documentary collections on immigrant naturalization are Edith Abbott, *Immigration, Select Documents and Case Records* (Chicago, 1924) and Philip Davis, ed., *Immigration and Americanization* (Boston, 1920). The rise of civic education is described in Charles E. Merriam, *Civic Education in the United States* (New York, 1934).

Philosophical commentaries on citizenship and democracy are Alexander Bickel, *The Morality of Consent* (New Haven, Conn., 1975), and Michael Walzer, *Obligations: Essays on Disobedience, War and Citizenship* (Cambridge, Mass., 1970).

DATE DUE
